Anishinaabe Mino-Bimaadiziwin

The Way of a Good Life

D'Arcy Rheault

Debwewin Press, Peterborough, Ontario

Data

Rheault, D'Arcy Ishpeming'enzaabid, 1963 -

Anishinaabe Mino-Bimaadiziwin, The Way of a Good Life / D'Arcy Rheault.

Includes bibliographical references.

For my parents, Gilles and Claudette

and my teacher Paul Bourgeois

Contents

Acknowledgements

I wish to extend my most humble appreciation to all the Elders and traditional Teachers who have taught me everything I know about Anishinaabe philosophy. I am also grateful to my graduate thesis supervisor, Edna *Asinii-kwe* Manitowabi (Odawa) and the members of my committee, Bryan *Washashkong* Loucks (Ojibwe), M.A. and Paul *Mishcogaboway* Bourgeois (Ojibwe), M.A. I acknowledge Brian *Waabishki Makwa* McInnis (Ojibwe), B.A. for all his comments on the initial draft of this project and Lillian *Biidawe'aandmod oo kwe* Osawamick-Bourgeois (Odawa) for helping me with the use of Anishinaabemowin.

I also wish to thank Dr. Joseph Couture (Cree/Métis) for sitting as my external examiner, and his permission to use some of his unpublished work and Dr. John Wadland for encouraging me to pursue a difficult subject. I am also thankful for Dr. Marlene Brant

Castellano's (Mohawk) permission to use her unpublished work and Helen [Bajorek] MacDonald for her exceptional editing skills.

I am indebted to Dr. Robert Malone, a kind man who believed in me before I knew how, Dr. Debabrata Sinha who pointed out an unseen signpost on my life-path, and Robert Gilmore for understanding all my personal twists. And finally, Robert Pirsig, for writing really great books.

Greetings

I extend my greeting to you. I hope that the time in which you read this work finds you in good health and spirit.

We are about to embark on a journey into the world of the Anishinaabeg and the Way of a Good Life. I hope that you read these words with care, understanding that I have chosen them to examine and explain many of the Teachings that I have received from Elders and traditional Teachers. It is also my hope that these words will contribute to a new understanding of the philosophical eloquence and depth of Anishinaabe thought and worldview.

Preface

I remember sitting in a coffee shop with a friend during the spring of 1993. It was a cool clear day. We were discussing the Undergraduate Philosophy Degree that I was about to complete that summer and of our plans for the future. At one point or another, our conversation turned to my aspirations as a young philosopher. I also remember telling her that I had recently become very curious about my Aboriginal ancestry.

I grew up in a typical middle-class French-Canadian family environment, with, I guess, typical middle-class French-Canadian values. I had even thought of becoming a Roman-Catholic priest when I was a teenager. My father's family first arrived from France in the early 1600's. My mother's father was from Québec and her mother from Northern Ontario. My maternal Grandmother was of Ojibwe ancestry that originated in Nipissing Territory.

Unfortunately my grandmother died when I was ten years old and I never had a chance to speak with her about our Ojibwe roots.

My mother' Aboriginal ancestry was always spoken of as something far back in the past, something that happened in the last century. And that's how it was as I grew up. My mother had never described herself as part Ojibwe, but rather only as a French-Canadian woman. As I sat there talking about my family history with my girlfriend, a peculiar thought sprang to mind, "I am part Native." This may sound like a simple conclusion, evident from my ancestry, but for me, at that moment, it was a completely new realization. Until *that* moment in time I had not thought of myself as being part Native. I'm still not sure why I started to talk about these things on that spring day.

At that point in my life I did not know any Aboriginal people. As I sat drinking my coffee I began to talk about the work that I would like to do in the future. Part of this work included learning more about myself as an Aboriginal person. I fantasized aloud about meeting traditional people, of learning the ceremonies and the various aspects of *their* worldview. But at that time I had no idea where these people could be found. In my mind, traditional Aboriginal people were a vanishing breed who had been assimilated into the larger American and Canadian culture. The media told me so, and I believed it.

I also spoke of my interest in examining Aboriginal philosophies from a philosophical perspective rather than an anthropological or ethnological perspective. I had recently read John (Fire) Lame Deer's book, *Lame Deer, Seeker of Visions* (1972), and was struck by the depth of his words. Unfortunately for me, I thought — as this book had been written in the early 1970's — that surely the traditional Aboriginal person no longer existed. Around the same time I also read Robert Pirsig's *Lila, An Inquiry Into Morals* (1991).

Robert Pirsig is famous for his first novel, *Zen and the Art of Motorcycle Maintenance, An Inquiry Into Values* (1974). This book overwhelmed me. I was nineteen when I first read it and I was at a complete loss to understand what he was saying on those pages. Initially this novel struck me as a simple travel-log, the story of a father and son on a journey of discovery as they crossed the great expanse of America in search of the Pacific Ocean. But throughout the novel Pirsig refers to his alter ego, Pheadrus. Pheadrus speaks of his process of learning, his questions about 'Quality' and 'Value'. He refers to various Western and Eastern philosophies; thoughts that were completely alien to me at that time. I was so captured by this novel that I must confess that it alone led me into academic philosophy. I consciously chose all my undergraduate courses, with Eastern Philosophy as my area of concentration, based on the issues and ideas that Pirsig wrote about in *Zen*.

It took eleven long years of part-time university study but finally, in the summer of 1993, at the age of thirty, I re-read *Zen* for what must have been the twentieth time. I finally understood the point that Pirsig was making in his book — that 'Quality' and 'Value' are the fundamental building blocks of reality and a belief that a subject/object system is necessary to understand the world is metaphysically faulty.

Pirsig's second novel, *Lila, An Inquiry Into Morals* (1992) has also had a profound effect on me. Among other subjects, this novel discusses many aspects of Aboriginal metaphysics which I had never thought of before. Very much like my experience with Pirsig's first novel, *Lila* captured my imagination. Intuitively I understood that this novel would lead me into graduate work. It is rather humorous to think that while I was discovering Pirsig's brand of Aboriginal metaphysics, I was also in the process of formulating a thesis proposal on a phenomenological examination of the Upanishads for my Masters Degree in Philosophy. I had found myself in the impossible position of thinking about Aboriginal philosophies while planning work in Eastern philosophy.

Not long after I started graduate studies I felt completely ambivalent about my work. I approached my thesis supervisor and asked for his counsel. After explaining my feelings to him, he told me that it was time for me to leave academic philosophy and pursue my own Aboriginal heritage. He was very supportive of my ideas to examine Aboriginal philosophies. He said simply, "We have taught you all that we can." With that I withdrew from the philosophy program and decided to enter Native Studies.

To my surprise, and I must confess my girlfriend's also, we ended up in Peterborough, Ontario, basically on a whim. We had visited earlier during the summer of 1994 and it just felt right. We moved and in the fall I began my classes.

The clearest memory I have of those first days at Trent University is sitting in the "Algonkian (Anishinaabe) Identity" course wondering what I was doing in Peterborough. I had spent many years struggling through my B.A. in Philosophy only to find myself at a new university effectively starting all over again by taking the pre-requisite undergraduate courses for a degree in Native Studies. My girlfriend had quit her job; we had both left our families behind and had found ourselves in a place where we knew nobody. All I could think of as I waited for class to begin was: "Am I crazy? My girlfriend is at home alone, we're broke, and here I am studying Aboriginal people." At that moment the instructor, Paul Bourgeois, entered the class. After introducing himself, explaining the structure of the course and encouraging us to introduce ourselves, one by one, he proceeded to give us a short lecture on the meaning of Anishinaabe identity. As I sit here looking at my notes from his first lecture I can't help but laugh a little. I only wrote down two things: 'Encourages the use of 'I' in essays' and the question he wanted each of us to answer at the end of the course, 'Who am I?'

Concerning the use of 'I' in essays, I was surprised to say the least. I had been trained in academic philosophy never to use 'I' in my papers. This was based, I was taught, on the fact that one should never include one's opinions or beliefs because the study of philosophy must be objective. And that "Who am I?" in my notes? To tell you the truth, I ended up spending a lot of time wondering about that. I wondered about my possible place in the Aboriginal world. In my mind I was a French-Canadian guy with some Aboriginal ancestry. Was there something here for me? Would I be considered another 'Wannabe': somebody attempting to be something they were not? Nobody had ever asked me who I was before, and I was curiously at a loss for an answer to 'the question.'

I received my first hint to the answer later that winter before Christmas. Paul Bourgeois invited me to his place in the country to observe a Sweat Lodge Ceremony. I arrived there with some tobacco, on the advise of a new friend, and I gave it to Paul once I entered his home. He accepted it and shook my hand. I was very nervous.

The rest of the evening is pretty much a blur, but I do remember a few things. I remember that it was very, very cold that night. The people who had come out to take part in the Ceremony where all standing around the fire as they were given the Teaching of the Sweat Lodge. After the Teaching, they undressed, and one by one they entered the Lodge. The heated rocks were put inside and the tarps were lowered over the doorway. After a few moments of speaking with the fire-keeper, I walked over quietly and tried to hear what was going on inside. All I could hear was the hushed whisper of people speaking. And then I heard a sound that has forever changed my life: I heard the Drum as the people inside the Lodge started to sing. I began to cry. Just like that. At that moment I felt like I had been away from my home for a very long time, unable to contact my family, and had finally found my way back. The experience was that intense.

It took a long time for me to understand what happened that night. I spent many hours with traditional Teachers and others discussing my emotional response to the sound of the Drum. Many told me that the Drum's voice has a way of awakening one's spirit, and that was perhaps what had happened to me. Perhaps. But I was still full of doubt and uncertainty about 'Who am I?'

The following spring I received an e-mail from Paul Bourgeois asking me if I would like to help with another Sweat. Unfortunately, I received the e-mail a day too late. I was very disappointed. I wrote back: "If you need help with another Sweat, please, please, please, call me on the phone." A few days later he did call and asked if I wanted to help. I was delighted and agreed. "There's only one thing," he said. "It's in Alabama." He explained that one of his students was Cherokee from Alabama and that he had asked him to go down and do a Sweat for his people.

A few nights before the trip I had a dream that I died in a terrible car crash. My sense of impending death was so intense that I made my Will when I awoke. A few days later (a little nervous) I left for Alabama to take part in my first Sweat. The expression 'Sometimes you have to travel far to find yourself' took on a lot of significance for me on that trip.

I remember clearly, as I sat in the damp, hot darkness of the Sweat Lodge in Alabama, of looking up and seeing the faces of dozens of old Aboriginal people looking in from above, as if the top of the Lodge was open. I could see them, old men and women, all leaning in to look at us. And they were all smiling. I intuitively recognized them as my ancestors witnessing the return of one of their descendants to the ancient tradition. I felt connected to my Anishinaabe family for the first time.

And that is how I started on this path. I have met those traditional Aboriginal people that I had dreamed of, and it is through them that I have discovered my Anishinaabe heart. My relationship with Paul Bourgeois has deepened over the past few years to such an extent that, as he has said to me, our respective roles as teacher and apprentice has evolved to a new level.

> The line between teacher and student becomes blurred sometimes when teacher and student become involved with teaching and learning. My involvement with D'Arcy Rheault is a good example of this occurrence. D'Arcy, initially was a student of mine in an undergraduate course, and later became an apprentice in our traditional culture. However, D'Arcy became a valued colleague in a mutual relationship of teaching and learning. In particular, D'Arcy was helpful in the many discussions on the

philosophical implications of Ojibwe Odewegewin [the way of the drum].

Paul has shared a great deal of his knowledge about Anishinaabe tradition and Ceremony and I have shared my knowledge of academic philosophy with him. Recently, I was deeply moved when I heard him describe our relationship as a "spiritual partnership." Since that first trip to Alabama we have travelled often together, and it is during those voyages, usually driving in the middle of the night, that we have discussed many important and profound ideas, many of which are now part of this book.

The people that have been central to my traditional education have all spent many years learning from the *Niswi-Ishkodeng Midewigaan* (Three Fires Midewiwin Society), a contemporary Anishinaabe spiritual society organized by Edward Benton-Banai in the late 1970's. I first attended the ceremonies of the *Niswi-Ishkodeng Midewigaan* in Bad River, Wisconsin in the spring of 1995. I spent four days sitting close to the ceremonial teaching Lodge listening to Chief Edward Benton-Banai recite and explain many Teachings. I have continued to learn from many people and this work is the result of that relationship.

This is only part of my story. The rest of this book reflects some of what I have learned since that trip to Alabama and those first Spring Ceremonies. It is incomplete, I am sure; nevertheless, it expresses the little I know about the depth and beauty of Anishinaabe philosophy and its impact on my life.

I must say that as I wrapped up the final research, about to begin writing, I became acutely aware of the process that lay before me. I felt completely unprepared for this project. I have only spent a very short time learning some of what I discuss in these pages since I came to the tradition later in my adult life. I approached one of my traditional Teachers for advise about writing this book and he told me to just take it easy, that everything would work out. So I've decided to relax and see what happens.

I have spent nearly three years researching and writing this book. I have discussed many traditional Teachings with Elders, traditional Teachers and apprentices. I have also asked them for direction in the research and writing of this book. In the fall of 1995 I went out and Fasted for two days for guidance in my academic work. In the end I found that my academic life and my personal life could not be separated. This realization led me to the conclusion that I must take personal responsibility for anything that I may write and discuss within these pages since these words come out of my own process of reflection. I am on a journey like all other beings. My life courses along a path set out for me by *Gzhe-mnidoo*; a life course I must discover from moment to moment. It is with this understanding that I began this journey, and it is also with this understanding that I accept the new knowledge that I am continually discovering about my own Anishinaabe culture.

This new knowledge is constantly coming to me. Even as I wrote these pages I continued to learn. My original rough draft has changed so many times that I have almost lost track of my original intentions. It seems that every time I sat down to continue my work, some new experience, Teaching or understanding would force its way to the front of my mind and spirit. I found myself perpetually re-writing my work, adding and removing whole sections. The title of this book, "*Anishinaabe Mino-Bimaadiziwin* (The Way of a Good Life)" came to me only as I was finishing my final draft. Originally, I intended to write a book on the epistemology of the Anishinaabeg, but something told me that I had to step further back to find a primary foundation. Initially, I thought of metaphysics but that didn't feel right either. I needed something from the Anishinaabeg and not the Greeks. Finally, I realized that I had to speak about my own life and my journey of learning rather than try to objectify Anishinaabe philosophy, as my academic training had taught me to do. This is not to say that these two methods are in opposition; rather, that an examination of Primary Experiential Knowledge precludes the necessity for a personal relationship with the knowledge that is being gathered and examined. This book, as an exercise of inquiry and examination is, of course, specific in-so-far as I make definite statements about what I have found. Yet, I never stand apart from this knowledge, objective and distant, for the sake of academically-defined methodological integrity. I am the knowledge I speak of — it forms the very being of my life.

The purpose of this work then is to examine and apply Primary Experiential Knowledge as a philosophical tool of exploration. This methodology is new in academic philosophy, as best as I can tell, since I am moving away from a traditional objective philosophical method. Research and learning for an Anishinaabe person includes more that an investigation of the external world. It also includes those revealed insights that happen within; insights that are presented as gifts by the Spirit, gifts that transcend the constraints of space-time. I am not talking about the usual steps in a rational investigation, like thinking about the Teachings or some empirical observations and finding commonality or conceptual order. Rather, I am speaking of the insight that has been given to me by my Teachers, particularly in my dreams, during my Fasting experiences and in Ceremony.

That is the scope of this effort: my own reflections on what I have learned. In the end, I can only speak for myself. *Mino-Bimaadiziwin* is the Way of *a* Good Life; therefore I only speak for one particular life: my life.

D'Arcy Rheault, *Ishpeming'enzaabid (Bizhiw)*

Peterborough, Ontario (Mississauga Territory), August 21, 1998

---

[1] Paul Bourgeois, "Odewegewin: An Ojibwe Epistemology" (Major Paper (draft), York University, March 31, 1998) TMs [photocopy], 3. (used with author's permission)

Introduction

I began this project in the fall of 1995. My intentions were simple enough: to examine Anishinaabe philosophy based on traditional Teachings. Early on, I envisioned a comprehensive document that would present various aspects of Anishinaabe worldview. I felt that this was necessary so that Anishinaabe philosophy could find its place with other world philosophies.

Earlier that summer, aware of the nature of my pending research and the scope of my work, I approached one of my traditional Teachers for some advice. He answered simply that I had to Fast[i] for my direction. He called this "Applied Anishinaabe Research". Initially I was confused by his use of the term research. I was aware that Fasting was designed to give a person a spiritual insight into one's identity and one's place in the world; but to describe it as research was new to me. Trained in academic philosophy, I had learned that research had to be an objectively systematic inquiry into a given subject in order to discover or elaborate on facts and theories. How being hungry, thirsty and alone in the 'bush' would constitute an objectively systematic inquiry into Anishinaabe philosophy was totally beyond me.

At this point, I feel it is necessary to describe my Fasting experience. Only then can my method and intention be fully revealed. This is a very personal subject for me; nevertheless, I believe this kind of discussion is important in showing that 'research means more than an examination of an 'objective' world.

I prepared for one month (one lunar cycle) before the *makadekewin* (the process of Fasting) began. Gradually, as I approached the day of *makadekewin*, I began to feel frightened and apprehensive of the physical and spiritual experience of going without food and water for two days.

One night, a week before my Fast, I experienced a *naapewewin* (vivid dream) in which I saw a *makadekewigaan* (Fasting Lodge). It was enormous, nearly three meters long and two meters wide. I stood before the *makadekewigaan* naked and very cold (which has been explained to me as the feeling of the unknown, of emptiness). As I opened the front flap and looked inside for warmth, I saw *Gchi-makade-makwa* (a large black bear). *Gchi-makade-makwa* looked out towards me, and without the use of the spoken word — rather a direct sharing of communication — told me to enter and that she would keep me warm. Without fear, I entered and *Gchi-makade-makwa* wrapped her great legs around me, and as I snuggled into her I fell asleep, warm and safe. When I awoke from my *naapewewin*, I immediately had a feeling of comfort and safety that allowed me to begin *makadekewin* without any hesitation.

The insight and revelations that I mention here are really gifts from *Manidoo* (Spirit). Some of the insights that I received from *Gchi-makade-makwa* were the shape and dimensions of my *makadekewigaan*, as well as the fact that I would be protected while I was out in the bush. I could have taken the usual steps in a rational investigation of what a Fasting Lodge is, and how it should be built, but I had been given my first lesson in Fasting directly from the Spirit of the great Faster herself, *Makwa*[ii]

I approached one of my traditional Teachers with this *naapewewin*, and he told me that it had been a good one, full of knowledge and insight into my reason for Fasting. He told me that I would find what I was looking for in my Fast, and that the answer would be definite and clear.

I went out a few days before my Fast was to begin, and built a *makadekewigaan* by myself. Although I had never built a Fasting Lodge before, I knew, by what I had been taught by *Makwa-manido*, how to go about it. I gathered the *wiigiwaamaatig* (Lodge poles) and placed cedar and hay on the ground as I had seen in the dream. I built the Lodge and covered it with a canvas tarp. I stood back when finished and was pleased to see the Lodge of my *naapewewin*. I returned to that Lodge for the next three days, sitting near it and reflecting on the purpose of my Fast. On the fourth day, I began my Fast. I used cedar to form a circle around the Lodge for protection and I entered inside. That first evening I fell asleep to the sound of people singing in the distance.[iii]

I slept most of the time I was in that Lodge, losing complete track of time. The next evening, a traditional Teacher came out to check on me, asking if I had seen or heard anything. I then told him of a powerful and moving experience that I had had the previous evening.

As I slept, I had a 'sense' that something or someone was circling outside of the cedar circle that formed a protective barrier around my Lodge. I could sense it, even though I was asleep[iv]. I then sensed that someone was trying to go under the cedar circle from the outside so that they could enter up inside my Lodge from underground. At that point I opened my eyes and saw *Makwa* emerge up from the ground at the eastern end of my Lodge. I immediately edged to the opposite side, sitting with my knees to my chest trying to protect myself. I remembered a traditional Teacher explaining to me that there was nothing that could harm me while I was in the 'sacred' place of my Lodge. I also realized, with some shock, that I was fully awake and that there really was a large black bear inside the Lodge with me. I was astounded; but at the same time, terrified, my heart pounding in my chest. I had never been this close to a bear before. In the complete darkness of that Lodge, Makwa was even darker, yet I could see her perfectly. I then heard her say without spoken word, but directly into my *O'de* (heart)ᵛ, that everything was going to be fine and that I would find what I needed. And then it was over; I just lay back down and fell asleep. As I told my traditional Teacher about my experience, he nodded and smiled. He then left and I re-entered my Lodge.

I spent the next day sleeping and gradually preparing the objects I had brought with me for when my traditional Teacher would return to get me for the Coming-out Ceremony. I did experience many other insights and dreams, but these will remain private.

This experience has completely altered my life. In fact, I did find everything that I needed to work on this book. In essence I have been shown the full dimension of *Kenjigadewin* (reality). I knew that any work that I would do would be done with the recognition of the insights, knowledge and gifts that were given to me by *Makwa-manido*. I also realized that I needed to approach a person of the Bear Clan and ask that person to be my main Teacher. A few weeks after my Fast, I approached Professor Edna *Asinii-kwe* Manitowabi and offered her my *asemaa* (tobacco) for her guidance in my work.

Over the past three years, I have had many other dreams and insights into my work. They have all come to me at times when I was unsure of my direction. I have shared this one experience with you to give an example of what I mean by 'more than an investigation of the external world.'

I struggled for some time with the idea of including this section in my work since it is taught that visions of a deep and personal nature should not be revealed publicly. This is done out of respect to the sacred character of the vision as well as ensures that gifts of spiritual insight are not used by a person in an inappropriate manner. At the same time, the knowledge that I have been given directly influences the scope of my work. Thus, with counsel from my traditional Teachers, and an intuitive sense that it is proper for me to do so, I offer this to you as an example of experiential learning through personal experience.

An Elder once told me that I am responsible for the Teachings and knowledge that I receive and that I must honour these gifts with respect. But he also said that what others do with the gifts of knowledge that I may share goes beyond my ability as a human being. Each is responsible for one's own personal actions and intents.[vi]

A Few Comments Regarding My Intentions

I have come to realize, through my involvement in Ceremonies and with Elders and traditional Teachers, that Anishinaabe conceptions of *Kenjigadewin* (reality) still remain true to the Original Instructions given by *Gzhe-mnidoo* (the Creator) and the traditions that have been passed down through countless generations. There are many Anishinaabeg who continue to share their knowledge and explore the complexity of Creation. But it is also appropriate to suggest that we live in a time when new generations of Anishinaabeg are gradually beginning to discuss their traditions in new ways.

There has been a long-standing conversation, perhaps even argument, amongst Aboriginal peoples concerning the writing of philosophy. Some are of the opinion that we should begin to share our various traditions and Teachings with others, while some are of the firm belief that any written discussion of philosophy or worldview amounts to a desecration of sacred oral Teachings. I wish to be clear: I find myself somewhere between these opposing groups. It is my firm belief that the time has come for the sharing of Anishinaabe philosophy, and I thank my Teachers for their encouragement in this matter. But my Teachers also have taught me that the sacred oral Teachings, because of their dynamic nature, must continue in an oral fashion in Ceremony so that their unique quality can be preserved. Thus, I intend to discuss the general philosophy that can be distilled or extracted from the traditional oral Teachings without reproducing those oral Teachings in written form.[vii]

I wish, from the outset, to make clear the serious limitations there are to revealing 'sacred' knowledge and even the personal learning I have done with regard to this knowledge in this book. The Teachings upon which I base this work are not here made available for the opinions and analysis of non-Anishinaabeg. It is taught that these people, unfamiliar with the ceremonial and cultural environment, cannot possibly 'feel' the power of these Teachings from these pages written in English. It is essential that these Teachings be experienced through the context and the protocol of traditional Ceremonies in the original language of the Anishinaabeg. This context and protocol includes, for instance, the place and time that the Teachings are given, who gives the Teaching, as well as the ceremonial presence of the Spirit of these Teachings. Without these aspects, the Teachings become static in presentation and meaning.

Throughout the writing of this work, I have been very aware of constantly wondering; "Can I say this? Am I revealing too much?" I have come to learn, through my Teachers, that there are subjects and issues that this kind of philosophical investigation — as good as the intention may be — could potentially interrupt, change, disturb and even irritate certain spiritual forces, places, and dimensions. These spiritual forces can be angered and even made vulnerable to the practices of some Native and non-Native peoples who like to borrow bits and pieces of various Aboriginal Traditions for their own personal use and gain. The spiritual reality that I have begun to learn about in my journey is indeed a beautiful and life-changing one; but, it is also an incredibly powerful one, not meant to be toyed with. For those who do not grasp the complexity of this context and protocol there is the very real possibility of mental, emotional, physical and spiritual injury. It is for this reason that I will not reproduce the oral Teachings in written form, and why I progress through this book with the greatest of care.[viii]

Nevertheless, I have found encouragement for this particular kind of project from Joseph Couture, a Cree-Métis scholar. In his paper "Native Studies and the Academy" he states that:

> The responsibility to interpret and apply the content of Tradition is a sanctioned enterprise. In the early 70's at the end of 12 days of discussion in a camp setting, summing up on behalf of Elders from Seven First Nations of Alberta in assembly, Elder Louis Crier stated:
>
> We would like to say that in order to survive in the 20th century we must really come to grips with the White man's culture and with White ways. We must stop lamenting the past. The White man has many good things. Borrow. Master and use his technology. Discover and define the harmonies between the two general Cultures, between the basic values of the Indian way and those of Western civilization — and thereby forge a new and stronger sense of identity. For, to be fully Indian today, we must become bilingual and bicultural. We have never had to do this before. In so doing we will survive as Indians, true to our past. We have always survived. Our history tells us so...
>
> So now, you younger ones, think about all that. Come back once in a while and show us what you've got. And, we'll tell you if what you think you have found is a moose.[ix]

This is what I have done and continue to do. My moose are the ideas expressed in this book. I have returned from time to time to my Elders and traditional Teachers to ensure that I had a moose in hand. Most of the time I did; many times I did not. This has been my process of learning and validation.

Method and Foundational Tenets

There are many issues that bound a discussion about Anishinaabe philosophy. Foremost is the need to situate this discussion within an intelligible framework that allows people not familiar with Anishinaabe thought to grasp the meaning of issues brought forward. It is also important that I describe and explain the methodology of my research so that it is clear that I am using a method of learning and sharing based on culturally recognized Anishinaabe protocols. With these introductory comments I hope that all readers, Anishinaabeg and non-Anishinaabeg alike, will be able to leave this experience with a new and deeper appreciation of a worldview that gives meaning and purpose to our lives and the way we, as Anishinaabeg, live.

As with any body of work, it is important to set out my method of inquiry and the source of this method so that the reader is able to have a point of reference from which they can examine what they read. The source of my method of inquiry is "Applied Anishinaabe Theory". Applied Anishinaabe Theory is a philosophical system that finds its foundation in the traditional knowledge that forms the nexus of Anishinaabe culture. This is based, in part, on the knowledge that everything (everyone) is alive and that we are all related. It is also based on an understanding that there are two aspects to reality: physicality and spirituality, and that they are ultimately two different expressions of one reality. These are primary truths as expressed by our Creation Story.

The method of inquiry used for this book is "Primary Experiential Knowledge". Primary Experiential Knowledge is set out as an epistemic system that finds its source in various aspects of knowledge. It is primary since it is the most basic form of knowledge upon which all other understanding is based, and it is experiential since knowledge comes out of one's interaction with the world. It is a process-oriented philosophical method interested in the theoretical and practical meanings of the metaphysics[x], epistemology[xi], axiology[xii], aesthetics[xiii], logic[xiv] and ontology[xv] of Anishinaabe *Mino-Bimaadiziwin* (the Way of a Good Life).

I feel that my method is the beginning of an active incorporation, recognition and use of one's own perspective as a critical source of inquiry and means of knowing. The sensing of the 'self' and my cultural intuition are what necessitate a different approach because in Anishinaabe philosophy this method is a fundamental way of knowing; a fundamental epistemology, the absence of which would render this study invalid. This method is about coming to objective truths through a subjective method of inquiry and analysis not explicitly characteristic of any Western systems, but of Anishinaabe culture. I have learned that it is not possible to separate myself from the world; I am a spirit walking in this world. 'Others' guide me in this world, but it is, ultimately, an individual journey. Thus, my method is a qualitative inquiry built on a blending of participant observation and participant participation[xvi] incorporating my thoughts, reflections, emotions, spirituality and actions in my personal learning.

Again we are reminded that this is a system of interconnection, consequently any discussion of theory and practice is artificial in its categorization. As an example of the difficulty of categorizing interconnected ideas and concepts, Paul Bourgeois (Ojibwe), in his examination of the drum as a source of knowledge and the role that the drum plays in teaching, concludes that:

> Emphasis on the individual's lived-ethical concerns in relation to the cosmos makes Odewegewin an "Onto-axiological Anishinaabe Epistemology," that is, an Anishinaabe system of knowledge that is based on the existential imperatives expressed by the quality of Creation. Nevertheless, there is a difficulty in creating these conceptual abstractions for various aspects of Anishinaabe worldview for the simple reason that terms like epistemology, philosophy and religion do not specifically exist in Anishinaabemowin, as we understand them in English. Yet, the concepts do exist, but not in isolation of each other due to the interconnected nature of the philosophical system.[xvii]

Primary Experiential Knowledge, thus, as an epistemic system, takes into consideration that there are various aspects of knowledge that are expressed in life. This is seen as the "Seven Directions"[xviii] of *Kendaaswin* (knowledge); namely, *Bzindamowin* (learning from listening), *Anishinaabe-Kendaaswin* (traditional knowledge), *Manidoo-waabiwin* (seeing in a spirit way), *Gnawaaminjigewin* (to look, to see, to witness), *Eshkakimikwe-Kendaaswin* (land-based knowledge), *Kiimiingona manda Kendaaswin* (the Original Instructions given to the Anishinaabeg by *Gzhe-mnidoo*) and *Manidoo-minjimendamowin* (spirit memory).

Primary Experiential Knowledge also recognizes that there are given assumptions or beliefs that must be acknowledged. Assumptions and beliefs are thorny issues in philosophy; nevertheless, they exist as a foundational structure within this method. Assumptions and beliefs are generally defined, in the West, as suppositions or opinions, something not immediately susceptible to rigorous proof. This definition can be misleading, potentially leading one to conclude that there is no rigorous system implied in my method. It is here that we have the first instance of confusion based in language. As Paul Bourgeois (Ojibwe) has discovered in his own work on Anishinaabemowin:

> I began to see a vertical and horizontal layering of concepts. I found ideas within ideas with parallel Teachings related to the other. Each [Anishinaabe] word and idea [was] independent and yet simultaneously dependent upon the other idea and

teaching for its meaning. In other words, it is within Anishinaabe thought and worldview that we find an interconnectedness that precedes language and behavior.[xix]

When English terms like 'assumption' and 'belief' are defined there invariably is a lexicological reference to their Greek and Latin roots, and as such, their meaning is directed by those traditions[xx]. In Anishinaabemowin the term for 'belief', and by association 'assumption' (as it would be categorized in English), is *n'debewetawin*[xxi]. *N'debewetawin*, on the surface, is translated as "My belief", but literally means "the truth that is evident in the way of the action." "In the way of the action" refers to the Primary Experiential Knowledge one gains when using a process-oriented method. And it is 'truth' that is evident, not 'opinion' or 'conjecture'. This understanding of the Anishinaabe meaning of 'belief' reveals some of the philosophical structures that underlie my method.

Human Beings and the 'Other'

For the Anishinaabeg, the aliveness of natural entities, what many Western traditions consider material objects, means that they have the same kind of consciousness, self-awareness and volition as a human being. The Anishinaabeg make a general assumption of consciousness in others based on the similarity that they have with human beings. It is essential that the definition of the 'other' be understood as being much broader than the standard Western definition.

The metaphysics and ontology of the Anishinaabeg place them in a large, all-encompassing social, physical, spiritual and environmental reality. Community is one of all life, all relations.[xxii] In other words, Anishinaabe worldview is concerned with the Being-structure of reality. The Anishinaabeg live in a world which is peopled not only with human beings, but also by persons and personalities that are other-than-human. In dreams and visions, for instance, these other-than-human persons are directly encountered, and develop a personal relationship with the dreamer and the vision seeker. The old people remember that:

> In the old days our people had no education. They could not learn from books or teachers. All their wisdom and knowledge came to them in dreams. They tested their dream, and in that way learned their own strength.[xxiii]

Even though the 'old days' are past, the underlying truth and reality of this quotation still exists for many Anishinaabeg. Joseph Couture (Cree/Métis), when discussing Aboriginal 'knowing' states that:

> A corollary to the issue of "knowing" is that of mysticism. From a Native spiritual standpoint, as I see it, mysticism is a question of becoming/being rooted or grounded in relationships with all constituents or dimensions of reality. I like Fox's description of mysticism because it is congruent with my understanding of Native spiritual experience. He

> holds that "... the essence of the mystical experience is the way we are altered to see everything from its life-filled axis, to feel the mysteries of life as they are present within and around us." That's Indian.
>
> To arrive at a direct experiential understanding of that definition is a primary learning task. To discover how ceremonies, for example, mediate helping energy and Teachings takes some doing. Prayer, ritual and Ceremony ground one in life....[xxiv]

This philosophical reality allows the people to find their place in a very complex world. It also allows the people to learn about that complex world, situating themselves directly in the web of Creation.

A Primary Experiential Knowledge method is a personal method. In essence, it is finding 'objective truth(s)' through a necessarily subjective method and process. In the case of research dealing with the Way of a Good Life, knowledge and identity, it not only develops the necessary structures for an investigation, but also ultimately provides a degree of self-revelation for the investigator. A. Irving Hallowell[xxv] explains that this "self-image" depends on the fact that:

> ... the world of personal relations in which the Ojibwa live is a world in which vital social relations transcend those which are maintained with human beings. Their culturally constituted cognitive orientation prepares the individual for life in this world and for a life after death. The self-image that he acquires makes intelligible the nature of other selves — human and other-than-human persons — for the

conceptualization of the latter presumes an essentially similar nature, with added power.

If we do not take the qualitative aspects of their world into account, the behavior of the Ojibwa cannot be fully understood or explained. The cognitive process of individuals — perceiving, remembering, imagining, conceiving, judging, and reasoning — are integrally related to the cognitive orientation that is derived from their culture. The "set", "the silent organization" which they possess as a consequence of their training, experience, and values, provides them with a part of the necessary psychological structure which enables them to function not only as human beings but as Ojibwa.[xxvi]

This foundational understanding is necessary so that the role Anishinaabe worldview has in developing a research method concerning identity, traditional knowledge, and other areas of study, can be fully understood. Paul Bourgeois (Ojibwe) remarks that:

Anishinaabe culture is Onto-Axiological. In asking what the cultural imperative is for Anishinaabe culture, I saw that it is concerned with what is good and ethical. The values and their metaphysical nature intertwined. The name of the Anishinaabe means, "the good male being, lowered to the Earth from the above, created from nothing." An Ojibwe Elder spoke at length regarding the idea of being good in relation to doing good. The nature of Anishinaabe Onto-axiology is a cultural imperative of Anishinaabe life, because it is concerned with the essence of the self in relation to ethical questions. It is a philosophy and an epistemology concerned with what is ethical in relationship to the essence of the self.[xxvii]

What follows is a deeply personal exploration of what I am still in the process of learning. In a way it may be seen as non-academic in the traditional academic sense due to the autobiographical nature of this work. However, I have used a traditional Anishinaabe philosophical method as a template from which to better distinguish the key components and concepts of this system. To some extent, this work consists of assumptions and beliefs based in part on Teachings but mostly on Primary Experiential Knowledge. I am fortunate that I have met and befriended some exceptional Anishinaabe traditional Teachers who have gently and lovingly shown me the path of life. And I am also very fortunate that those Teachers cared enough to allow me to explore that path on my own (with a few directions on the way).

I offer this not as the final word, but simply as an attempt to encourage an ongoing, and in some cases, a new discussion. I am not a traditional Teacher. I am only an apprentice in the early stages of learning the complexity of Anishinaabe thought. My personal experience (both spiritual and cultural) has been so liberating that I only wish to share what I have learned. I do not want to be seen as an authority in Anishinaabe philosophy. The real authorities are the Elders and traditional Teachers. Paul Bourgeois (Ojibwe) explains that:

> Many hours are spent listening to these Teachings in Ceremony, and repeated seasonally over one's life. Carried with the Teachings are values, principles,

> attitudes, and codes for Bimaadiziwin. A significant aspect central of an Anishinaabe worldview is faith, belief and understanding of a parallel spiritual realm. Having an appreciation and respect for the existence of a spiritual reality supported by faith and belief is necessary then.[xxviii]

I must also stress that I am not a fluent speaker of the Anishinaabe language. Any Anishinaabe terms used in this book come from conversations with many fluent speakers, especially Lillian Osawamick-Bourgeois (Odawa), Brian McInnis (Ojibwe) and Prof. Edna Manitowabi (Odawa). It is these discussions which first revealed to me that many philosophical answers could be discovered when Anishinaabe terms are 'unpacked'.

I am constantly reminded in my dealings with fluent Anishinaabeg that a worldview is only accurately, or fully perhaps, accessible to Anishinaabemowin speakers who have the Teachings and who are 'schooled' in this system of traditional life — who interactively associate and commune with the land in their daily life. Thus they are reminded daily of respect and humility, because we as humans forget so easily when we live in vast impersonal cities. Very few Anishinaabeg have the complete intersection of these realities simultaneously in their everyday life.

It is also necessary that I prepare the reader for my use of repetition. Repetition is a vital component of oral traditions. Throughout the life of a person, one may hear a Teaching one hundred times or more. Each time the Teacher will accentuate different parts of the Teaching to 'bring out' a new or complex philosophical aspect. Gradually, there is a refinement of the 'thought' of the Teaching. I will also re-visit many concepts and ideas throughout these pages and, as I progress through this story, there will be an ongoing refinement of thought.

Finally, I have decided to use the term Anishinaabe (g) as a general term for various Nations of people related by common traditions, history, language and ancestry rather than the often used Ojibwe (Chippewa) — only one Nation among many.[xxix]

Since Anishinaabe philosophy is based on interconnection it is very difficult to isolate various aspects of this worldview into neat and tidy chapters. Thus, I have decided to divide this book into two parts: "Traditional Knowledge, the Academy and a Spiritual Renaissance" and "Anishinaabe: The Good Being." Part one, which is in essence an extended introduction, examines some foundational tenets of Anishinaabe philosophy in order that a general context for examination is presented. I also discuss the traditional educational methods of the Anishinaabeg and the role of Native Studies in the development and implementation of a culturally-based method that remains true to traditional protocols, but also, necessarily, uses academic methods in projects such as this book. I have also included a short chapter on the Spiritual Renaissance that Aboriginal peoples have experienced in the last 30 years. I feel that this chapter is necessary to show that Aboriginal peoples are continuing the discovery and investigation of traditional knowledge. There has been an incredible growth in various Aboriginal traditional philosophies and spirituality in the last few decades and this has led directly to a general re-emergence of the intellectual traditions (the *Chinshinabe*[xxx]) that are key components of Anishinaabe societies.

Part two examines various aspects of Anishinaabe epistemology, metaphysics, axiology, and aesthetics in a more detailed manner. The last chapter *"Eyaa'oyaanh"* is devoted to an examination of identity. At its core I attempt to answer the question: "What does it mean to be an Anishinaabe person?"

I see the various sections of this book as circles within a larger circle. Moreover, like a circle, it does not matter where I begin because I will eventually return to my starting place. So it may appear that I am wandering from topic to topic but I am like the little boy who, long ago, went out on a spiritual search. He wandered to the Four Sacred Directions before he found himself back where he started. In the end, he found the Way of a Good Life where it had always been — at home.[xxxi]

Notes

---

[1] Fasting (*Makadekewin*) is a ceremonial undertaking that involves abstinence from water and food for a number of days. It is traditionally used as a step in the life of a young person towards adulthood. In my case, I Fasted for two days in Ennismore, Ontario (fall, 1995) and for four days at Petroglyph Provincial Park, Ontario (spring, 1998).

[2] Traditional Teacher, conversation with author, 1998. For the Anishinaabeg, the bear is known as "the Great Faster", a medicinal spirit due to the long periods of hibernation they experience every winter. Within the word *Makadeke* there is reference to *Makwa* (bear), and *Makade* (black). (Throughout this book I will not reference, by name, the traditional Teachers and Elders that I have spoken with. I do this in accordance with the accepted Anishinaabe protocol that explains that traditional knowledge does not belong to one person alone. To attribute any traditional knowledge to one person, by name, would give the impression that that person alone was the authority and/or owner of a body of knowledge that, for lack of a better word, 'belongs' to a culture.)

[3] Traditional Teacher, conversation with author, 1998. During the Fast, members of the community come at sundown to sing ceremonial songs and celebrate the person Fasting and to help her/him gain strength for the Fast. It is also done to help the Faster call for the spirits. This singing is done in recognition that the gifts received during a Fast are gifts for all the community to share.

[4] I can best describe this as a lucid dream.

[5] When I say that she spoke directly into my heart, I mean that there was immediacy to the experience. It was not linguistic in the usual sense; rather, a kind of awareness that overcame me.

[6] Elder, conversation with author, 1997.

[7] Edward Benton-Banai has written some of the oral tradition of the Anishinaabeg. In the event that I do refer directly to the tradition, I will use *The Mishomis Book, The Voice of the Ojibway* (Wisconsin: Indian Country Communications, 1988).

[8] Traditional Teacher, conversation with author, 1998.

[9] Joseph Couture, "Native Studies and the Academy", in *Indigenous Knowledge in Global Context: Multiple Readings of Our World*, ed. George Dei, Buod Hall and Dorothy Goldin Rosenberg (Toronto: University of Toronto, forthcoming, 1998), TMs [photocopy], 3. (used with author's permission) (emphasis added)

[10] Metaphysics is a branch of philosophy that deals with the study and interpretation of reality.

[11] Epistemology is a branch of philosophy that deals with the study and definition of knowledge as well as the process of knowing.

[12] Axiology is a branch of philosophy that deals with values, ethics, aesthetics, and religion.

[13] Aesthetics is a branch of philosophy that deals with the study of beauty in nature and art.

[14] Logic is a system of reasoning that is used to develop correct and reliable inferences applicable to any branch of knowledge or study.

[15] Ontology is a branch of metaphysics that studies the nature of being or existence.

[16] "Participant participation": term coined by Brian McInnis, conversation with author, 1998.

[17] Bourgeois, "Odewegewin: An Ojibwe Epistemology", 14-15. Paul Bourgeois uses the term *Odewegewin* (the Way of the Drum) as the conceptual framework for his investigation of Anishinaabe epistemology. My use of the term *Mino-Bimaadiziwin* closely relates methodologically to *Odewegewin*. However, due to the interconnected nature of Anishinaabe philosophy, Paul decided to focus on the Drum as a symbol of Anishinaabe theory and practice. I have chosen *Mino-Bimaadiziwin* due to the autobiographical nature of this work. The holistic nature of Anishinaabe philosophy leads to a curious situation in the methodology of investigation. No matter where one starts, or what one decides to speak about, in essence it is all the same subject: Creation.

[18] See Figure 2

[19] Paul Bourgeois "An Ojibwe Conceptual Glossary." (Major Glossary Paper (draft), York University, February 26, 1998) TMs [photocopy], 7. (used with author's permission)

[20] For instance, the Greek philosopher Plato, in his attempt to explain the structure of the world, posited a "two world metaphysics" whereby there was a distinct division of sensual and intellectual matters. He believed that there was a hierarchy of knowledge with conjecture and belief in the realm of the sensual (physical) world and knowledge (what he called belief based in fact rather than opinion) and wisdom in the realm of the intellect. This system clearly separates matter of the body (the sensible) and matters of the mind (the intellectual) into distinct categories. This categorization began a tradition in the West of distinguishing between the 'mind' and the 'body' as distinct and separate 'things'.

[21] Related to this is r-*debwetaan*: "I believe it." Both of these words have *debwe*: truth, correctness, at their root.

[22] See Figure 3

[23] Anonymous Elder (Chippewa), 1929, in *Native Wisdom*, ed. Joseph Bruchac (San Francisco: HarperSanFrancisco, 1995), 68.

[24] Joseph Couture, "The Role of Native Elders: Emergent Issues" in *The Cultural Maze: Complex Questions on Native Destiny in Western Canada*, ed. John Friesen (Calgary: Detselig Enterprises, 1991), 212.

[25] I have attempted to draw, from the field of Anthropology, quotations that agree with the over-all knowledge that I have gained in the past years. The fact that I include non-Native writers in this bookdoes not imply that they have a better working knowledge of my culture, rather that their ideas run parallel with Anishinaabe knowledge. It is also interesting to note the use of the past tense by some non-Native writers when discussing or explaining contemporary Aboriginal cultures. In referring to Native writers, I will reference their nationality.

[26] A. Irving Hallowell, "Ojibwa Metaphysics of Being and the Perception of Persons" in *Person Perception and interperson Behaviour*, ed. R. Tagiuri and L Petoullo (California: Stanford University, 1958), 79.

[27] Bourgeois, "Odewegewin: An Ojibwe Epistemology", 43-44.

[28] Bourgeois, "An Ojibwe Conceptual Glossary", 7.

[29] See Figure 1

[30] See Chapter 3, *Chinshinabe*

[31] Edward Benton-Banai, *The Mishomis Book, The Voice of the Ojibway* (Wisconsin: Indian Country Communications, 1988), 87.

Chapter 1

Worldview as Philosophy

To see beauty is to seek the truth with an open/not empty mind.
To hear beauty is to share in the creation of harmony.
To feel beauty is to experience the world with a kind heart.
To taste and smell beauty is to touch the joy of life.
To speak and act in beauty embraces the mysteries of light into darkness and darkness into light.
To walk in beauty is to dream/dance on the road of the heart.

Washashkong, 1998

The recognition of Aboriginal worldviews as philosophical systems is a very recent progress in the academic environment. There is a slow but gradual movement within academic circles to include the knowledge and worldviews of Aboriginal peoples in conversations; particularly concerning the environment. Nevertheless, we must also remember that there is currently only one Native Studies Ph.D. program in North America (U. Arizona (1996)) with a second beginning at Trent University in 1999.[i] There is still a long way to go before Aboriginal philosophies are academically and socially recognized as valid and valuable sources of knowledge.

In the past (and in some cases even today) discussions concerning Aboriginal cultures were relegated to the sphere of anthropology and by relation, ethnology. This, in part, was due to ethno-centric beliefs held by the dominant societies of North America with regards to Aboriginal peoples. As a result of systematic governmental policies of genocide and assimilation, the late 19th century saw a vast army of anthropologists and ethnologists enter into 'Indian Country'. They recorded and catalogued the cultures and rituals of what were then considered the 'vanishing Indians' of the Americas. Anthropological and ethnological research of the late 19th and early 20th centuries was mainly concerned with the collection of the material culture of Aboriginal peoples. The vast number of Aboriginal artefacts found today in public and private collections all over the world attest to this fact. There was also a fascination with various Aboriginal ceremonies, rituals, music, cultural stories, scrolls and sacred objects (e.g., Barnouw 1944; Densmore 1907, 1910, 1932; Chamberlain 1913; Hallowell 1926; Hoffman 1888, 1889, 1891; Mallery 1894; Michelson 1892; Radin 1928; Raudot 1770; Reagan 1914, 1927, 1933; Schoolcraft 1860; Waugh, 1919). Non-Aboriginal anthropologists and ethnologists, with varying degrees of accuracy, described the ceremonies and rituals they witnessed or even those they only learned of second-hand.

There was also an early tradition of publication by Aboriginal authors with the best examples being William W. Warren's *Oral Traditions Respecting the History of the Ojibwa Nation* (1860) and *History of the Ojibways, Based Upon Traditions and Oral Statements* (1885), A. J. Blackbird's *History of the Ottawa and Chippewa Indians of Michigan* (1887) and Arthur C. Parker's *The Indian How Book* (1927).

The latter part of the 20th century has seen Aboriginal writers begin to publish work in areas of philosophy, politics, culture and spirituality, to name a few (e.g., Benton-Banai, 1988; Cardinal, 1991; Colorado, 1988; Couture, 1972, 1978, 1979, 1982, 1987, 1989, 1991, 1997; Deleary, 1990; Deloria Jr., 1973, 1979, 1995; Dockstator, 1993; Dumont, 1976; Johnston, 1992; King, 1983; Loucks, 1990; Mohawk, 1985, 1990, 1991, 1992, 1994; Momaday, 1968; Sinclair, 1994; Williams, 1991; Warrior, 1992). Modern Aboriginal writers strike me as 'Indian and shameless'[ii] while early Aboriginal writers tended to mask their identity or have only a limited tie to the Aboriginal people they wrote about. Perhaps they were trying to be 'objective' in their study. Today it seems that many Aboriginal writers are saying what they do because they have a genuine knowledge of their respective culture and language — such perspectives only possible to actual insiders.

Even though there is an increasing inclusion and recognition of Aboriginal philosophies in academic circles, this alone does not characterize these systems as distinctly or predominantly philosophical. Philosophical thought has been at the heart of Aboriginal societies since time immemorial. There have always been philosophers amongst the people. The Anishinaabeg have a tradition of intellectuals called the *Chinshinabe*. They are the Elders and traditional Teachers who are the caretakers of cultural and sacred knowledge. They take on the responsibility of maintaining the flow of *Nebwakawin* (wisdom) that passes from generation to generation. As Joseph Couture (Cree/Métis) states:

> I'm of the opinion that Elders are superb embodiments of highly developed human potential. They exemplify the kind of person which a traditional, culturally based learning environment can and does form and mould. Elders are evidence that Indians know a way to high human development, to a degree greater than generally observable in prevailing Western society. Their qualities of mind (intuition, intellect, memory, imagination), and emotion, their profound and refined moral sense, together with a high level of spiritual/psychic attainment, are perceived as clear behavioral indicators, deserving careful attention and possible emulation.[iii]

Anishinaabe Philosophy and What It Means

This book, to put it simply, is concerned with Anishinaabe philosophy. In particular, I am concerned with the axiological aspects of this philosophical system; in other words, values, ethics and to a lesser extent, aesthetics. Concerning Anishinaabe philosophy as a whole, it is, I believe, important that I indicate some of the central foundational ideas of this system so that there is a general context to work from with regard to the content of this work. I do not mean to suggest that it is possible to summarize all aspects of Anishinaabe metaphysics, ontology, epistemology, etc. into a few sentences, but there are some key philosophical tenets that must be expressed so that this work can have contextual integrity.

First and foremost, as Paul Bourgeois (Ojibwe) writes, is the understanding that:

> The Anishinaabeg have no term for [the separation of] man/nature, or [this] subject/object dichotomy in their language, because there is no nature, or environment, as such, understood to be separate from the self. In my initial research in the [Anishinaabemowin] dictionaries I did not find words for art, philosophy, mind, and knowledge. There certainly is religion, art and philosophy in Anishinaabe life. However, they exist as abstract nouns. What I am talking about is a completely different worldview, a worldview where we relate and interconnect everything with a manido (spirit) dwelling within everything [iv]

A belief in *Gzhe-mnidoo*[v] is also fundamental to Anishinaabe philosophy. Existence is Creation and the Creation Story of the Anishinaabeg sets out the process and purpose of this physical reality. In Basil Johnston's (Odawa) words:

> Because Kitchi-Manitou[vi] [is] a being existing in the supernatural sphere, this spirit [is] super-ordinate to human experience, knowledge and description. But it [is] taken for granted and accepted as true that Kitchi-Manitou created the universe, the world and the beings upon, above, and below, both corporeal and incorporeal, from a vision or dream. Creation, by which the mystical vision was brought into the realm of physical reality, [is] seen as an act of generosity and a sharing of the manitou's goods with those in need.[vii]

The Anishinaabeg have received Original Instructions from *Gzhe-mnidoo*, instructions that are used to guide the people through life. Anishinaabe oral history speaks of the creation and lowering of the first human being to this Earth and a migration from the East (Atlantic Ocean) to the Great Lakes region (and not a west to east migration over the Bering Straight)[viii]. Humans were the last beings created and placed on Earth, and we are referred to as the weakest and most dependent in Creation.[ix]

There are ancestral prophecies that foretold of the coming of Europeans and the conflict that would arise with the arrival of this 'new visitor'.[x] There are also strong prescriptions for the Way of a Good Life and how we as humans should behave toward our relations. This relationship is based on the view that all life is related; whether mineral, plant, animal and/or spirit. There are detailed Teachings about the Clan system and one's role in life depending on one's name, sex, age, experience, and about family structures.[xi]

Anishinaabe philosophy is a philosophy of interconnection. Creation is understood as both the source and unity in movement of all life. This holistic perspective is at the very heart of my system of inquiry and explanation. This book aims to isolate and explain some of the philosophical aspects of this system, despite the recognition that such divisions are artificial to the perceived understanding of the Anishinaabeg.

There are detailed oral Teachings about all these subjects, and the skin of an onion metaphorically symbolizes them. When we look at the onion we see it as whole; but, in fact, we are only looking at the surface. If we remove this skin we find another deeper down. Remove this one and another is below, and so on. Anishinaabe philosophy is very much like the onion. The more one learns the more one finds, and the process continues, going deeper and deeper, all through one's life.[xii]

Traditional Education and the Academy

Anishinaabe tradition already has an educational method as part of its structure. In traditional and contemporary times the Elders and the traditional Teachers are the ones who guide the apprentice on his or her path of learning since the education of an Anishinaabe person happens throughout the lived-experience of that person. Joseph Couture (Cree/Métis) explains this when he states that:

> The doing that characterizes the Native Way is a doing that concerns itself with being and becoming a unique person, one fully responsible for one's own life and actions within family and community. Finding one's path and following it is a characteristic Native enterprise which leads to or makes for the attainment of inner and outer balance.[xiii]

The Elders and traditional Teachers are the embodiment of the traditional education system used by the Anishinaabeg. They are the teachers in the school of life.

When reflecting on these aspects of traditional education and learning I become aware that a possible difficulty with my method of Primary Experiential Knowledge within the framework of a Western academic system is, as has been remarked on by Vine Deloria, Jr. (Sioux), that:

> Regardless of what Indians have said concerning their origins, their migrations, their experiences with birds, animals, lands, water, mountains, and other peoples, the scientists [i.e., Western academics] have maintained a stranglehold on the definitions of what respectable and reliable human experiences are. The Indian explanation is always cast aside as a superstition ....[xiv]

I believe that it all comes down to a misunderstanding of the Anishinaabeg's conception of the inter-subjective nature of Creation. In the West it is generally taught that there must be a detachment from the research in order that the work be objective. Understandably, this caution is based on a general fear of research becoming relativistic and purely subjective.

The West has already been exposed to relativists like Protagoras (fl. 450 B.C.E.), an ancient Greek philosopher, who defined knowledge as that which is relevant and more so only relevant to one person's individual tastes.[xv] Protagoras stated, "Man is the measure of all things, of those that are that they are, of those that are not that they are not."[xvi] He is referring to the individual with all the qualities, negative and positive, pertaining to that person. Thus, as far as Protagoras was concerned, what one knows is not some objective reality that is the same for all people; it is a reality particular (relatively speaking) to only one person at a given moment. One perceives something and its significance changes from moment to moment as one's own tastes change. As such, relativism is the view that truths and values vary from context to context, and person to person.[xvii]

In comparing the differences between Western and Aboriginal methods of research, Vine Deloria, Jr. (Sioux) explains that:

> The major difference between American Indian views of the physical world and Western science lies in the premise accepted by Indians and rejected by scientists: the world in which we live is alive. Many scientists believe this idea to be primitive superstition and consequently the scientific explanation rejects any nuance of interpretation which would credit the existence of activities as having partial intelligence or sentience. American Indians look at events to determine the spiritual activity supporting or undergirding them. Science insists, albeit at a great price in understanding, that the observer be as detached as possible from the event he or she is

> observing. Indians thus obtain information from birds, animals, rivers, and mountains which is inaccessible to modern science. Indians also know that human beings must participate in events, not isolate themselves from occurrences in the physical world.[xviii]

This difference is also apparent when we examine the structures of universities. Couture (Cree/Métis) characterizes universities as places where people strive for success in the eyes of their peers. This success is based on a "rule-and-conquer syndrome"[xix] which affirms that: "You meet academic standards, as we define them. You meet these standards via the strategies which we also define. That is the road to success."[xx] It is an "ethos [that] is essentially colonizing, subjugating, controlling."[xxi] Couture (Cree/Métis) concludes that this process is understandable due to the "mechanistic rationalism"[xxii] that prevails in universities.

Conversely, my method entails a personal inter-subjective exploration of the physical-spiritual world. "It is difficult," Couture (Cree/Métis) states, "for many intellectuals, so encased in their academic egos to perceive what is extraordinary reality [the physical-spiritual world] — in this case, that "what" which traditional Indians see, and that "how" whereby they arrive at seeing the "what."[i.e., extraordinary reality.][xxiii] The "how" is often not so disturbing to "academic intellectuals" as is the "what." It is the "what" which always seems so completely impossible and illogical because it is outside the realm of the quantifiable.

A purely rational or analytic approach itself is "half-brained"[xxiv] as Couture (Cree/Métis) puts it. The framework chosen for my study asserts that it is essential that the pursuit of knowledge happen from the perspective of a whole person. "[The analytic approach] needs to be complemented by the intuitive faculty."[xxv] This is what Couture (Cree/Métis) calls "full-mindedness"[xxvi,] the union of mind and heart, of intellect and intuition.

The traditional system of education for the Anishinaabeg has always been one of apprenticeship (with human and non-human beings). The knowledge that is received through apprenticeship is not relative to the opinions and tastes of the receiver, but is verified and acknowledged by a system of Elders, traditional Teachers and *Enadizewin* (Natural Law). But this is not a repudiation of the place of individual perspective[xxvii.] The Anishinaabe system of knowledge is a vastly complex system, with built-in protocols and processes that one must follow in order that one places oneself within an appropriate and valid epistemic context. Couture (Cree/Métis) notes the nature of such apprenticeship in describing the system as one which is:

> ... comprehensive in scope — its focus is health, (physical, emotional, mental, spiritual) — balance and harmony within and without with all things, life forms, Nature and the Cosmos. Through apprenticeship the laws of Nature are learned; it facilitates entrance to other levels of consciousness, to additional ways of knowing.[xxviii]

This is, for all intents and purposes, scientific knowledge.[xxix] Pam Colorado (Oneida) explains that:

> For a Western-educated audience the notion of a tree with spirit is a difficult concept to grasp ... [i.e.,] the universe is alive. Therefore, to see a Native speaking with a tree does not carry the message of mental instability; on the contrary, this is a scientist engaged in research![xxx]

This Primary Experiential Knowledge method strives to achieve exactly this kind of research: metaphysical certainty through already existing structures of Anishinaabe metaphysics, ontology, axiology and epistemology. It is, as Couture (Cree/Métis) notes:

> ... a question of discovering through direct experience that there are entities on other planes, entities which are not of the realm of illusion, or hallucination. It is learning to become quiet, "attentive" as Black Elk says. It is a question of entering into Indian psychic areas, and of learning to live by Indian rules of time and space, such rules are none other than universal, cosmic or "natural" laws.[xxxi]

The Role of Native Studies

Native Studies is in itself an academic discipline, yet it is one that is characteristically meta-disciplinary. As Joseph Couture (Cree/Métis) states in his discussion paper, "Native Studies, Some Comments":

> Native Studies strives as responsibly as it can to present a way of perceiving and expressing these

relationships (self, others, family, community and to the Cosmos), in fresh and novel ways perhaps, always congruent with authentic traditional processes and values. This demanding responsibility stipulates equally an able and sure grasp of contemporary conditions, together with a conscious experiential sense of the core or characteristic spiritual dynamic of Native life philosophy, in order to render, intentionally and systematically, a valid translation of culture-based knowledge, skills, and attitude. In other words, Native Studies seeks to develop a culture-rooted sense of both worlds in all their dimensions, in time and space, and to do so today in a bicultural mode.[xxxii]

Couture (Cree/Métis) continues by explaining that the 'ground' of Native Studies can be better appreciated when certain key assumption are presented and explained. The assumptions that he outlines are first that "it is believed that Native Studies, because of its roots in Aboriginal world view, can and does present a philosophy that unifies learning,..."[xxxiii] i.e., that it is meta-disciplinary. Corollary to this is the fact that Native Studies seeks to "demonstrate the inherent validity and usefulness of a heritage and philosophy ... which images visions, and voices "And all our relations, ..."[xxxiv] Second it "can and does bring an ancient understanding that learning leads to development of mind and attitude, and adaptation in conduct."[xxxv] Native Studies as one facet of "North American Aboriginal Tradition, seeks to express a deep, comprehensive perception of all reality as sacred, and hence sacralized, ..."[xxxvi]

A contemporary Aboriginal person, even of mixed heritage like myself, must, as Couture (Cree/Métis) tells us:

> ... consider certain insights and skills as necessary to successfully function in a bi-socio-cultural system. It is imperative then that such a person be or become intuned insightfully both to the spiritual and psycho-cultural nature and requirements of traditional survival and enrichment, as well as to the exigencies and shaping influences of the dominant, director culture(s).[xxxvii]

Further to this, this new culture-based reality is producing a new breed of Aboriginal intellectuals. Paul Bourgeois (Ojibwe) and Dan Longboat (Kanienkehaka) explain that the academic world is gradually seeing the emergence of what they call the "Indigenist"[xxxviii]:

> An Indigenist is an Indigenous person (although not exclusively) who combines the abstract and theoretical thinking involved in the creation and transmission of Indigenous knowledge. However, the conceptual and sometimes ethereal qualities of Indigenous thought for the Indigenist does not remain in the mind, but is lived on a daily basis. The Indigenist is clearly a thinker and practitioner of Indigenous knowledge. I have heard this expressed by many different Elders that this was our culture, something that had to be lived. In Anishinaabe society there have always been the metaphysicians and philosophers who concerned themselves with mental activity, and they were usually the medicine people, prophets, and spiritual leaders. This tradition of intellectual/spiritual activity has not easily transferred itself into the current way of doing things in western society. Learning by doing, in many Indigenous

societies is the basic tenet of learning. Experiential learning is the key aspect of Original Experiential Research. Discovering what was already known as true is an essential principle for acquiring knowledge in Anishinaabe life. Therefore, we learn by doing and discovering what we have come to know to be true for ourselves.[xxxix]

The discovery of what was already known as true is a system of affirmation and revelation. Different aspects and degrees of what is true are revealed to each person, each seeker. Paul Bourgeois (Ojibwe) goes on to explain that:

> Indigenists are needed to review and analyze what has been written about us, to clear the mind of inaccurate representations made in these texts. The Indigenist is also needed to write their own-stories regarding their origins, migrations, and cosmological understandings of the universe.[xl]

Absolutes and Reality

When I explain the role of insights and knowledge from a spiritual source, I am, of course, assuming that that spiritual realm is real and approachable. My understanding of Creation and *Gzhe-mnidoo* is one that speaks of the absolute oneness of reality. Indeed, I am speaking of absolute truths and an absolute reality. Traditional Teachings and traditional Teachers have been quite clear on this point, and through the development and growth of my Primary Experiential Knowledge, I not only believe, but *know* with certainty that the truth, as evident in the way of the action of Creation, is absolute. I share this same view with other traditional

Anishinaabeg who follow the traditional protocols that I use. Not exactly the usual words and sentiments of an old academic philosophy major, but this does bring us to one of the fundamental problems of discussing the appropriateness and validity of my approach: academia's apprehension of absolutes. According to Couture (Cree/Métis):

> Universities are apprehensive of absolutes, and become very nervous about the intellectual vice of absolutism, for its experience, in the sciences, the humanities, and the social sciences, is with the ambiguous, the tentativeness of theory, the shortcomings of method and inquiry.
>
> Universities are wary — their task is to question assumptions. Indeed, it is vital to a university's sense of fulfillment of mission that it can question assumptions. Because of that, from this relationship to and with each other, i.e., Native Studies and the University, a standing and necessary tension ensues — the inclination to verbal articulation and restraint vs. an ancient and intractable world-view that is silent, energetic and generous, that experiences all reality as sacralizing, that prized metaphor, intuitive imaging, together with higher order mental prowess. In a sense therefore, of both parties is required an ecumenical approach to each other, a willingness to find in traditions other than its own, other subsets of learning, other understandings, other valid interpretive systems.[xli]

I believe that I am an example of this ecumenical approach. As a person of Ojibwe and French-Canadian ancestry, a traditional person and an academic, I straddle both worlds, able to gain and express from both. We are witness to a unique time when the old is becoming new; we are rediscovering the underlying texture of Anishinaabe and other Aboriginal philosophies.   As Couture (Cree/Métis) explains:

> ... at present, Tradition, manifest in its many tribal expressions, is being rediscovered, investigated and reclaimed, and Native Studies is one of the key players in that pursuit.[xlii]

Without repeating what has already been stated, I think that identity, traditional knowledge, cultural revitalization, and education are at the very core of the method that I use in my work. Edward Benton-Banai (Ojibwe), the Grand Chief of the *Niswi-Ishkodeng Midewigaan*, explains that at present we are beginning to see the results of a movement by Aboriginal peoples to reclaim their self-identity and to revitalize Aboriginal cultures.   Edna Manitowabi (Odawa) has called this a "Spiritual Renaissance"[xliii]. Chief Benton-Banai (Ojibwe), in *The Mishomis Book, The Voice of the Ojibway*, states that:

> The prophet of the Seventh Fire of the Ojibway spoke of an Osh-ki-bi-ma-di-zeeg' (New People) that would emerge to retrace their steps to find what was left by the trail. There are Indian people today who believe that the New People are with us in the form of our youngest generation.   This young generation is searching for their Native Language. They are seeking out the few elders who have not forgotten the old ways. They are not finding meaning to their lives in the Teachings of the American society.   They are searching for an understanding of the Earth as Mother of all things. They are finding their way to the Sweat

Lodges, Spirit Ceremonies, Drum Societies, Midewiwin Lodges, Pipe Ceremonies, Longhouse Meetings, Sun Dances and Kivas that have survived to this day. This younger generation is discovering the common thread that is interwoven among the traditional Teachings of all natural people.[xliv]

This approach allows Aboriginal people, who are sensitive to complex traditional knowledge systems, to investigate the world in a more complete manner. By exploring a traditional method of learning and ultimately using it in research, the identity of a person is expanded and expressed in a traditional way. Rather than using only a Western system of research, we must use an Anishinaabe system for Anishinaabe worldview, an Ongwehónwe system for Ongwehónwe worldview, a Lakota system for Lakota worldview, etc.

In the end we must realize that the assumption that Aboriginal worldviews can be adequately explained by a totally alien western worldview is the essence of imperialism. As Benton-Banai (Ojibwe) explains, there are still Elders and traditional Teachers out there who are well learned in traditional knowledge systems. In order that this method, or any Aboriginal method of research, is comprehensive and rigorous it is imperative that the Elders and traditional Teachers be sought out and learned from. It is with their guidance that today's Aboriginal peoples will be able to retrace those steps necessary to find what was left by past generations on the side of the trail; that is, learning about, and actualizing traditional education, identity, knowledge and ultimately, cultural revitalization. Couture (Cree/Métis) explains that:

> In that way, once again, Elders and Tradition are primal givens. Our perceptions and grasp thereof can and do shape and influence our response to contemporary realities. This knowledge elicits an ethical attitude and response. Traditional viewpoint claims a "right" vision as conditional to seeing and understanding life in the "right" way.[xlv]

Using such a method, Aboriginal peoples will then be able to examine and base their lives on the traditional Teachings of their respective cultures, rather than only the teachings of the dominant society. There is no doubt that Aboriginal peoples will continue to share this land with Euro-Americans and other immigrants, but we are now beginning to realize that we do not have to base our lives on the values and structures of that dominant society. This method allows a process that is rooted in tradition and traditional learning, a process that allows a development of identity, traditional knowledge and cultural revitalization, as well as a model for a more inclusive system of education.

Primary Experiential Knowledge and Research

I do not advocate a separation of Aboriginal peoples from the university environment. I am in agreement with Joseph Couture's (Cree/Métis) opinion that we can find a balance between academic methods and traditional methods, thus developing a system of education that is equitable and valuable to all.

> At a minimum, I think that the education of students in Native Studies must involve a very personal, critical reflection not only on one's knowledge, but also upon one's experience of self, others, and social contexts, for these are necessary to the fullest possible participation in a bicultural life context.[xlvi]

I believe that this approach is appropriate in relation to research in Native Studies since it expands on the initial aim of Native Studies: the study of Aboriginal peoples. Moreover, Native Studies is not limited to an objective study of Aboriginal peoples as separate objects of study. Native Studies also includes Aboriginal people as active researchers. I also believe that this method can and should be used in all academic disciplines so that a broader investigation of the world can take place. As we have seen, research for some Aboriginal people includes more than an investigation of the external world. It can, and many times is, a personal journey of self-discovery of what it means to be Aboriginal. When I first entered Paul Bourgeois' course on Anishinaabe Identity in 1994, I knew very little about my Anishinaabe heritage. It is through this academic university course that I first discovered a part of myself that until then was unclear, and it is through this experience that I found my traditional Teachers. When I began to learn about Anishinaabe tradition, unlike an anthropologist or ethnologist, I did not distance myself objectively from the ceremonies and their Teachings, I embraced those Teachings and made them part of my life. Only in this way was I able to discover and internalize the necessary basis for this kind of examination.

Notes

---

[1] There are no Philosophy Ph.D. programs in Aboriginal philosophies (although Lakehead University, Lakehead, Ontario, now offers a Master of Arts degree in Native Philosophy). Aboriginal people interested in studying Aboriginal philosophies must still, essentially, develop their own methodologies and approaches within broad 'interdisciplinary' or 'multi-disciplinary' programs. Perhaps the day will arrive when a person like myself will be able to obtain a Ph.D. in one of the many varied Aboriginal Philosophies, rather than a Ph.D. in Environmental Studies or Native Studies.

[2] Brian McInnis, conversation with author, 1998.

[3] Joseph Couture, "Next Time, Try an Elder!, 1979", TMs [photocopy], 7. (used with author's permission)

[4] Bourgeois, "An Ojibwe Conceptual Glossary", 9.

[5] Gzhe-mnidoo: (compound word) Gchi-zhe-manidoo; Great and Kind Spirit.

[6] Kitchi-Manitou: the Great Spirit.

[7] Basil H. Johnston, forward to *Dancing with a Ghost, Exploring Indian Reality* by Rupert Ross (Ontario: Octopus, 1992), x.

[8] See chapter 2, "Anishinaabe".

[9] Benton-Banai, *The Mishomis Book, The Voice of the Ojibway*, 3.

[10] Ibid., 94-102.

[11] See Edward Benton-Banai, *The Mishomis Book, The Voice of the Ojibway* for a general account of the history of the Anishinaabeg.

[12] Traditional Teacher, conversation with author, 1996.

[13] Couture, "The Role of Native Elders: Emergent Issues", 207.

[14] Vine Deloria Jr., *Red Earth White Lies* (New York: Skribner, 1995), 19.

[15] G.S. Guthrie, J.E. Raven and M. Schofield, *The Presocratic Philosophers, A Critical History with a Selection of Texts*, 2d ed.,(Cambridge: Cambridge University Press, 1983), 411.

[16] Ibid.

[17] Ibid.

[18] Deloria, Jr., *Red Earth White Lies*, 55-56.

[19] Couture, "Next Time, Try an Elder!", 12

[20] Ibid.

[21] Ibid.

[22] Ibid. (passim).

[23] Ibid., 12-13.

[24] Ibid., 13

[25] Ibid., 12-13.

[26] Ibid.

[27] See chapter 3, Absolutes and non-singular Truths

[28] Couture, "Next Time, Try an Elder!", 13.

[29] The English word 'science' finds its root in the Latin 'scientia', meaning metaphysical certainty.

[30] Pam Colorado, quoted in *Words of Power, Voices from Indian America*, ed. Norbert S. Hill, Jr. (Oneida), (Colorado: Fulcrum, 1994), 26.

[31] Couture, "Next Time, Try an Elder!" 14.

[32] Joseph Couture, "Native Studies, Some Comments", April 1, 1993, TMs [photocopy], (Native Studies, Trent University, Peterborough, Ontario), 3. (used with author's permission)

[33] Ibid.

[34] Ibid.
[35] Ibid.
[36] Ibid., 5.
[37] Ibid.
[38] Paul Bourgeois and Dan Longboat, conversation with author, 1998.
[39] Bourgeois, "Odewegewin: An Ojibwe Epistemology", 10.
[40] Ibid., 63.
[41] Joseph Couture, "Native Studies, Some Comments", 6-7.
[42] Ibid., 13.
[43] Edna Manitowabi, conversation with author, 1997.
[44] Benton-Banai, *The Mishomis Book, The Voice of the Ojibway*, 111-112.
[45] Couture, "Native Studies, Some Comments", 14.
[46] Couture, "Native Studies and the Academy", 11.

Chapter 2

A Spiritual Renaissance

We didn't know for a long time that we were equal. Now, we know, and there's no stopping us anymore. We had forgotten our Story. Now, we're starting to understand.

Traditional Native Axiom[i]

There was a period of time when many Aboriginal ceremonies were hidden throughout North America. This was due to a concerted attempt by the dominant Canadian and American governments to stop all Aboriginal ceremonies and to integrate the people into mainstream society. Ceremonies were banned, from the Midewiwin in the East, the Sun Dance in the Prairies and the Potlatch in the West, to name a few.[ii] Vine Deloria, Jr. (Sioux), reminds us that in the United States:

By the time of the Allotment Act of 1887 (Dawes Act), almost every form of Indian religion was banned on the reservations. In the schools the children were punished for speaking their own language. Anglo-Saxon customs were made the norm for Indian people; their efforts to maintain their own practices were frowned on, and stern measures were taken to discourage them from continuing tribal customs. Even Indian funeral ceremonies were declared to be illegal, and drumming and any form of dancing had to be held for the most artificial of reasons.[iii]

With the passing of the Indian Reorganization Act (1934), Aboriginal people who happened to live within the boundaries of the United States were allowed religious freedom. "Traditional Indians could no longer be placed in prison for practising old tribal ways."[iv] But the price for this so-called freedom was the destruction of traditional tribal governments and their replacement with Bureau of Indian Affairs (BIA) organized governments, as well as the re-allocation of tribal lands, which saw most reservations cut in half or more.[v] This 'reorganization' created "... corporate forms of government for political and economic ends, [which] created the same problems of religious confusion in the Indian tribes that existed in America at large."[vi] Further, was the ever-increasing encroachment of non-Native populations onto isolated lands. Deloria, Jr. explains that:

One of the primary aspects of traditional tribal religions has been the secret ceremonies, particularly the vision quests, the Fasting in the wilderness, and the isolation of the individual for religious purposes. This type of religious practice is nearly impossible today. The places currently available to people for vision quests are hardly isolated. Jet planes pass overhead. Some traditional holy places are the scene of strip-mining, others are adjacent to superhighways, others are parts of ranches, farms, shopping centres, and national parks and forests.[vii]

In Canada there was also a concerted attempt to put an end to Aboriginal ceremonies and cultural societies. Katherine Pettipas (Cree) reminds us that:

> In 1885, the Canadian Government outlawed the ceremonial distribution of property through potlatches and other forms of religious expression practiced by many Northwest Coast Aboriginal cultures in British Columbia by amending the Indian Act of Canada. Subsequent modifications to this legislation (1895) allowed the federal government, under the auspices of the Department of Indian Affairs, to undermine certain religious practices among other Aboriginal Cultures. In particular, certain rituals associated with the Sun (or Thirst) Dances were prohibited, as were giveaway ceremonies involving the massive distribution of goods. Over the years, other legislated regulations were introduced in support of a more general level of religious repression as well as locally imposed government restrictions on cultural behaviour that went "beyond the law."[viii]

She also points out that:

> Giveaways at ceremonies held by the Midewiwin, or the Grand Medicine Society, were also subjected to surveillance. In 1925, a number of Saulteaux from Craig Lake, Saskatchewan, were dispersed while attempting to conduct a Midewiwin Ceremony. Since the offering consisted of material goods, the Ceremony was considered to be a breach of Section 149

[Amendment 1914: Indian Act 1876]. During the same year, two other men were arrested on similar charges; both were found guilty but were released with a warning.[ix]

One of the ways the federal governments tried to destroy Aboriginal cultures was through the imposition of a dominant form of education. Pettipas (Cree) explains that:

In 1879, residential "manual labour" school system as it had been developed in the United States by American educators such as Richard Pratt, the Director of Carlisle Indian School at Carlisle, Pennsylvania was adopted [in Canada]. It was hoped that, by removing young children from the influence of their parents and relatives, they would become effective emissaries of Christian civilization among their own people. The ramifications of this educational system for Indians was that assimilation would not be a matter of choice, but would be imposed on them by the dominant society.[x]

These governmental policies against Aboriginal traditional ceremonies and cultural ways were legislated due to the fact that:

Government officials and missionaries contended that certain indigenous religious practices were immoral and seriously undermined the assimilative objectives of Canadian Indian policy. However the rationale for adopting coercive measures against indigenous religions had much deeper roots, ... [it was] based on a belief on the part of the Department officials — and it was correct — that there existed a direct connection between indigenous worldview, ceremonial life, and the social, economic, and political structures of the community.[xi]

It is important to remember that the oppression of Aboriginal ceremonies and cultural ways was imposed on the Aboriginal Nations without discussion or negotiation with those people. Pettipas (Cree) notes that:

> While arrangements for land cessions and economic assistance were made through a treaty-making process, federal regulations regarding the administration of Indian concerns were unilaterally imposed. The authority and sweeping powers of this Indian administration were defined in regulations contained in the Indian Act of 1876 and its amendments. These regulations were developed to transform "Indians" into "Canadians" through a colonial relationship characterized by wardship and tutelage.[xii]

All these laws and resolutions only succeeded in confusing and disturbing traditional governments and ceremonies. And yet there was a prophecy that had circulated around Indian Country, the traditional homelands of the Aboriginal peoples of North America, for many decades. It was said that the people would begin to search out their Elders and traditional Teachers again when the Eagle flew to the highest place. On July 20, 1969, everybody watched on television as Apollo 11 landed on the moon, and heard those men send the message "The Eagle has landed."[xiii]

The Aboriginal Spiritual Renaissance that began in the late 1960's and early 1970's was characterized by young Aboriginal people leaving their homes and venturing throughout North America to seek Elders and traditional Teachers. Couture

(Cree/Métis) recalls that, "Amazingly and concurrently, and virtually everywhere in North America, signs of revitalization appeared."[xiv] Some Anishinaabeg travelled from the East to the Smallboy and Mackinaw camps in Alberta, the Rolling Thunder camp in Nevada as well as Wyoming and other western states and provinces. In many cases people experienced their first Fasting and Sweat Lodge Ceremonies. They were beginning their Spiritual quest for their traditions.

After years of travelling and seeking Elders, many were told that the answers that they sought could only be found back where they came from. In his examination of the return to the Traditions by Aboriginal peoples, Couture (Cree/Métis) remarks that:

> By the late 60's Aboriginal peoples around the world began to discover inspiration and means to obviate and move away from oppressive, devastating influences. To their unabated astonishment these discoveries were made in their respective backyards.[xv]

For the first time many realized that the Teachings relevant to their lives could only come from within their own cultural traditions. Many people from the East did find the beginnings of their spiritual path with the Arapaho, Plains Cree and other Western Nations for example, but they were shown that their original Teachings were to be found at home. Gradually people began to question the 'pan-Indian' idea, the idea that all Aboriginal people are the same, that there is only one Aboriginal worldview.

An Odawa woman from Ontario remembers her search experience in the early 1970's when she discovered her traditions in her own Nation's territory.

> When we went out for those first ceremonies in 1974 they were in Michigan. We came on to them quite by ... well ... I don't want to say by accident, because I don't think it was by accident. We were supposed to be going to Native Awareness Days in Marquette, Michigan at the University there. The students were putting on a weekend gathering and by the time we got there things were pretty well over. There was one lonely Tipi sitting out on campus and that was it. Everybody else was gone. So we were kind of wondering what to do and I saw a little flyer, a small card, and there was a picture of a Waterdrum and it was on a huge bulletin board in the Native Studies Lounge and right at the bottom, right at the bottom of this bulletin board with all these papers was a little card. What caught my eye was a picture of a Waterdrum and with the stones and the way it was tied because I had never seen one like that before. And it talked about Ojibwe ceremonies and it was south of there and it was that weekend. So this was Saturday morning, Saturday noon, around there, and rather than come all the way back home I ... there was just a strong pulling sensation with that drum, that picture of the drum. I said to J. "I think we're supposed to go here. These Ojibwe Ceremonies, let's go check them out. They're just over here." It was about a two-hour drive actually. So we drove down there. ...
>
> For me it was ... whenever I come on to things like that I look for other signs too. I noticed a lot of hawks that time. Incredible. The other thing was that sense that there was something special that was about to unfold. There was a very strong sense about that. When we

got there we kept following these signs, and most of them where ribbons or cloth eh? [laughs] And we got to this camp and I guess for me it was hearing somebody speak Ojibwe. Somebody speaking the language, that was one, that was for me very special. We set up camp. There was a gathering that evening. And so I saw that Waterdrum there. That was when we first met E. (an Anishinaabe Elder). For me, I don't really remember too much about what went on in terms of their Ceremony because there was just this incredible sense of coming home, I had come home to something that I had been yearning for, for a long time and so I just sobbed. Every time that Waterdrum sounded and they were singing songs, I sobbed. I sobbed and sobbed. It was like an old, old Spirit finding something that was, that had been ... I had been waiting for a long time. So there was that sense. So every time that they sang a song, that's the way it was, like there was a waterfall. So it was quite cleansing for me, quite an emotional experience for me. I didn't really understand what had happened that time.

So ever since then, ever since that first experience we went to ceremonies after that. It was the sound of the drum. And there were only a few people there.[xvi]

Many people who went out in those early years express the same feeling: that of coming home. Paul Bourgeois (Ojibwe) remembers:

When I first heard the Waterdrum, I had a profound experience that would affect my life for years to come. When I went up to St. Charles and heard the Waterdrum, it was like I had come home for the first time. The sound of that drum was like I knew inside that my people, my ancestors, parents had done that forever. I knew that I belonged to that drum and that

> it belonged to me. So I knew I had found what I was searching for. What I was looking for all those years, was connected with that drum and with those Teachings that I heard and those songs and everything that was being done.[xvii]

When I reflect on the short history of our Spiritual Renaissance I am astounded by the fact that so many individuals went searching at the same time and that most tell of the profound impact the sound of the drum had on their lives. Paul Bourgeois (Ojibwe) explains that:

> This experience with the Odewegan [drum] is widespread for Aboriginal people when they came into contact with Odewegan for the first time.[xviii]

As people sought their respective Elders and traditional Teachers they began to realize that:

> ... the "constants" for "living a good life" are carried by a timeless traditional reflection, continuously renewed down through the ages. What-is-carried, in its essence, manifests as process principles such as spiritual awareness and values development, and expresses as constituents underlying a continent-wide variety in language, customs and ways of First Nations, understood as paramount to "loving-life", as engendering patterns of connecting responses to self, others, family, community, and the Cosmos. The "stuff" of relationships reveals as the "ground" to Aboriginal being and becoming, and provides a sure footing, a step at a time, to the necessary walk into and through contemporary dilemmas.[xix]

This is what those people came to find, evidence that the traditions still existed. Many believed that all was lost and forgotten, and they were astonished to find that the old people still carried out their sacred duties. The search was difficult because almost all ceremonies and Teachings had gone underground, due to the oppressive nature of the dominant society in North America. Many Elders were very suspicious of new people who came to them, and many had decided years before to stop holding public ceremonies for reasons of safety for their families and communities.

> In the late 1960's, triggered by a sudden, strong wave of seekers, Elders, although flattered and grateful, were initially flustered and were forced initially to rethink and redefine themselves and their roles. They were faced with dire and unsettling questions about identity and survival, and with the basic paradoxes regarding the nature of the Native world and the fundamental issues about the world in which humans live.[xx]

Nevertheless, the small trickle of Aboriginal people who went in search of their cultures quickly became a deluge. By the mid-1970's hundreds, if not thousands, of Aboriginal people of every Nation were travelling about America looking and waiting for signs to direct them. Spiritual gatherings, Socials and Powwows became the main source of information about traditional Lodges, Teachers, where people had been, and what they had found.

I have heard the stories of people from Ontario meeting other people from their community or Reserve by chance in remote teaching camps in Alberta, or at Fasting camps in Wyoming. I have also seen people, as they tell one another the stories of their search, come to realize that that they had missed each other by only a few days or weeks, 25 or 30 years before, in places like Michigan, Manitoba and North Dakota.

These early years also saw the development of A.I.M. (the American Indian Movement) and a new cry for justice throughout Indian country.[xxi] The American Congress, in 1978, passed a Joint Resolution entitled the American Indian Religious Freedom Act (1978) to address many issues that came out of the American Indian Movement's (A.I.M.) activities in the early 1970's.[xxii] Nevertheless, "... the federal courts have since ruled that the resolution did not protect or preserve the rights of Indians to practice their religion and conduct ceremonies at sacred sites on public lands."[xxiii] Even in the past few years there have been reports of Aboriginal peoples being harassed for wearing certain feathers as part of their traditional dancing regalia. While I was in Cherokee territory in Alabama in 1996, I heard a story of a little boy forced to remove his dancing regalia in the middle of a Powwow in Mississippi by Federal Agents because he had wild turkey feathers attached to his bustle.

In Canada, even though the last recorded interference in ceremonies such as the Midewiwin, "resulted in the prosecution of George Gilbert of the Wabigoon Reserve, Ontario, in 1938,"[xxiv] the history of religious and cultural repression and the rights of Aboriginal peoples to religious freedom remains an important issue today. Pettipas (Cree) reminds us that:

Even after the regulations were deleted from the 1951 Indian Act, many elders and ritualists remained fearful of performing their ceremonies openly, and some continued to believe that the laws against their ceremonies were still in effect.[xxv]

In both the United States and Canada the issue of Aboriginal religious freedom, to this day, remains unresolved.

Of particular note are concerns over the access to and use of religious objects held in museum repositories; the protection and use of sacred lands and sites in the face of development; the right to practice indigenous forms of religious expression within the prison system; the transport of sacred materials across state, provincial and international boundaries. In the United States, The American Religious Freedom Act (albeit inadequate) was passed in 1978 to protect Aboriginal religious freedoms, and, in Canada, the protection of Aboriginal cultures is a major issue in the ongoing discussions on self-government occurring between the federal government, the provinces, and the First Nations.[xxvi]

Many of the Anishinaabeg who went out and searched for their Teachings nearly thirty years ago are today the Elders and traditional Teachers of our communities here in the East and elsewhere. They are also the parents of a new generation of Anishinaabeg who are being raised within their respective traditions in sober and healthy homes. It seems impossible that so much could have been accomplished in so little time (not forgetting that a great deal more needs to be done) and many of the people have reawakened from a very long slumber.

Nevertheless. it is also true that some are still dozing, but their brothers and sisters are gradually awakening them.

The Spiritual Renaissance of Aboriginal peoples all across Turtle Island[xxvii] has also been an Intellectual Renaissance. The People are gradually recognizing the rigorous intellectual traditions inherent in traditional Knowledge. This intellectual tradition of inquiry and discussion is central to Anishinaabe philosophy and as an expression of one of the main tenets of *Mino-Bimaadiziwin* (The Way of a Good Life) is the focus of what follows.

Notes

[1] Couture, "Native Studies and the Academy", 5.
[2] Vine Deloria, Jr., *God is Red* (Colorado: Fulcrum, 1994), 212, 240, 246-47, 268-69 (passim), and Katherine Pettipas, *Severing the Ties that Bind: Government Repression of Indigenous Religious Ceremonies in the Prairies* (Manitoba: University of Manitoba Press, 1994), 4-41 (passim).
[3] Deloria, Jr., *God is Red*, 240.
[4] Ibid., 240.
[5] Ibid., 6.
[6] Ibid., 212.
[7] Ibid., 246-47.
[8] Katherine Pettipas, *Severing the Ties that Bind: Government Repression of Indigenous Religious Ceremonies in the Prairies* (Manitoba: University of Manitoba Press, 1994), 3.
[9] Ibid., 157.
[10] Ibid., 38.
[11] Ibid., 3.
[12] Ibid., 17.
[13] Michael Thrasher (Métis), Workshop, Elders and Traditional Peoples Gathering, Trent University, Peterborough, Ontario, Canada, 1995.
[14] Couture, "Native Studies and the Academy", 2.
[15] Ibid.
[16] Edna Manitowabi, interview by author, May 1997, Peterborough, Ontario, tape recording.
[17] Bourgeois, Odewegewin: "An Ojibwe Epistemology", 46.
[18] Ibid., 47.
[19] Couture, "Native Studies and the Academy", 2.
[20] Couture, "The Role of Native Elders: Emergent Issues", 202.
[21] See Vine Deloria, Jr., *God Is Red, A Native View of Religion* (Colorado: Fulcrum, 1994) An excellent overview of the Aboriginal political movement in the early 1970's.
[22] Deloria, Jr., *God is Red*, 23-39 (passim).
[23] Ibid., 268
[24] Pettipas, *Severing the Ties that Bind: Government Repression of Indigenous Religious Ceremonies in the Prairies*, 157.
[25] Ibid., 7.
[26] Ibid.
[27] North America.

Chapter 3

Anishinaabe

There are a few people in each of the tribes that have survived to this day who have kept alive their teachings, language, and religious ceremonies. Although traditions may differ from tribe to tribe, there is a common thread that runs throughout them all. This common thread represents a string of lives that goes back all the way to Original Man.

Edward Benton-Banai,
The Mishomis Book, The Voice of the Ojibway

When the Anishinaabeg lived along the coast of the Great Salt Water there came to them Seven Prophets that warned of the future and the coming of a 'New People' from across the water in the East.

> When the seven prophets came to the Anishinaabe, the nation was living somewhere on the shore of the Great Salt Waters in the East. There are many opinions about where this settlement was. It is

generally agreed that the Ojibways and other Algonquin Indians were settled up and down the eastern shores of North America. We have some idea of the size of the nation from these words that were handed down: "The people were so many and powerful that if one was to climb the highest mountain and look in all directions, they would not be able to see the end of the nation."

There was an active exchange and communication among all the groups of people. They used the waterways of the land to travel by canoe. They had a system of overland trails. They used sleds and dog teams to travel in the winter. Life was full for the people here. The Clan system and its government were strongly enforced. There was ample food from the land and sea, and there were fish from many rivers.
[i]

The Prophets that had come to the people brought seven predictions of what the future would bring. The First Prophet told them "If you do not move you will be destroyed."[ii] Many people did not want to move their families on a migration to the West. Others where ready to do as the Prophets had advised them. And others decided to remain in the East to protect the Eastern doorway of the Anishinaabe Nation from the Newcomers.

They were called the Wa-bun-u-keeg' or Daybreak People. Today, it is speculated that these were the people living on the East Coast of Canada that the French called the Abenaki. ... It would come to pass that most all those who stayed behind, including the Daybreak People, were destroyed or absorbed by the Light-skinned Race at the coming of the Fourth Fire.[iii]

The Migration of the Anishinaabe from the Great Salt Waters in the East (the Atlantic Coast from the Canadian Maritimes down through the Carolinas) to the Great Lakes region began long ago.[iv] As the people spread west along the St. Lawrence River into what is now Southern Ontario throughout the northern and southern parts of Lake Superior and into present day Michigan, Wisconsin, Minnesota and Montana, they moved about and began their lives in new territories. Some people moved into Northern Québec and Ontario as far as Hudson Bay and others as far south as present day Oklahoma and some west to present day British Columbia, and south-west into Northern California and Northern Mexico.

The Anishinaabe language family is the largest in North America. It includes many Nations with a common history who speak a similar language with linguistic roots which can be traced back to the Atlantic Coast.[v]

Spiritual History

The Anishinaabeg that lived along the East Coast had been there since the time of the Great Flood. It is difficult to put a time frame on how long ago this was. It is possible to say that they were there for thirty thousand or even one hundred thousand years, or much more, but ultimately this temporal quantification only leads to a misunderstanding of the reality of the

Anishinaabeg. With reference to an Aboriginal sense of history, Vine Deloria, Jr. (Sioux) explains that:

> ... even the closest approach to the Western idea of history by an Indian tribe was yet a goodly distance from Western historical conceptions. What appears to have survived as a tribal conception of history almost everywhere was the description of conditions under which people lived and the location in which they lived. Migrations from one place to another where phrased in terms of descriptions of why they moved. Exactly when they moved was, again, "a long time ago."[vi]

The Anishinaabe Creation Story with the lowering of the First Good Being to Turtle Island, the Great Flood and subsequent migration is beyond the constraints of space and time. By this I mean to say that the Creation Story is spiritual in nature. This idea of spirituality with reference to history is something that is misunderstood by non-Aboriginal peoples.

When the Anishinaabeg speak of their history they include both temporal and spiritual aspects. Using my own life as an example, I have been alive for 36 years but my spirit has no age since my spirit exists outside of the constraints of time and space. This is a very difficult concept to grasp since we experience life mainly from a spatial-temporal perspective. It is 9:00 a.m. as I write this. I have worked on this project for nearly three years. This, and more, is my temporal reality, but ultimately there is no time, no before, now and after. These terms are used to quantify physical reality in order to provide us with the impression that we understand the world around us. Spirit is not spatial or temporal. And ultimately any understanding of this is beyond any linguistic description and perception.

I first became aware of this a few years ago when I began attending Sweat Lodge ceremonies. It is invariably explained that the present, the 'now', is circular, that is, that there is neither beginning nor end. Circularity — what James Dumont (Ojibwe) describes as a 360-degree view of the world[vii] — extends beyond the limitations of space-time in such a way that it reveals the "seven directions of the present."[viii] Time, as a circular reality, does not have a linear construction; i.e., past in the past and future in the future. Paul Bourgeois (Ojibwe) explains that:

> Being outside space-time is not necessarily a new concept (theory) for Anishinaabe people. This understanding is in the Teachings and practices of the Anishinaabe people. For example, the Vision Quest [Fasting], which marks the transition from boyhood to manhood in traditional Anishinaabe societies, is a place where young men have gone since time immemorial. The vision quest, for the Anishinaabe, is travelling into another realm or dimension, that is outside of ordinary space and time as we understand it, within our ordinary life experience. This realm for Anishinaabe people is understood as the "spirit world." An example of this understanding relates to time. The Anishinaabe understand that in the spirit world one-half second could be one-year in the ordinary physical realm, and one-minute could be a week, and so on. Spatiality and temporality do not exist in the spirit world. The spirit world, which is outside space-time, as we ordinarily understand it, is

not the purpose, in itself, or the destination of a Ceremony.[ix]

Manidoo and the Great Mystery

Spirit, although spoken of as individual spirits or *Gzhe-mnidoo*, is neither many nor one. "How is this possible," you may ask? If there is neither many nor one then there must be none. Essentially this is the answer. This is the Great Mystery of Creation. I am able to speak about Creation and all those created, I am able to speak of *Mino-Bimaadiziwin*, knowledge and identity but I speak of nothing. The first man, the one that was called Anishinaabe, came to be from nothing.[x] He exists as a non-being and gives existence and meaning to everything. It is true that he was created from a union of the four parts of Mother Earth,[xi] yet this spiritual reality exists within a non-temporal, non-spatial dimension. He is still with us today and yet never existed at all in the conventional sense of space-time. Ultimately, an Anishinaabe ontology does not exist; neither does a definitive metaphysics, epistemology or axiology. These are my conceptual projections on the non-existence of reality. At this point I am sure that you are scratching your head thinking: "What is this guy talking about?" To tell you the truth, I'm not too sure myself. In essence, I am trying to describe a reality that is non-describable based on my personal experience.

The idea that spirit precedes culture, language, thought, experience and even time is something that the Anishinaabeg hold as fundamental knowledge. When referring to *Mino-Bimaadiziwin* it is understood that the spirit is the essence and the way of being. I am a spirit having a human experience. It is, as Paul Bourgeois (Ojibwe) states, "onto-axiological."[xii] The term onto-axiology explains the quality of existence; i.e., the good. The Way of a Good Life is more than a process or way to live. It is the underlying reality of existence that the term onto-axiology attempts to express. The Anishinaabeg are the Good Beings and they trace their ancestry back to the First Good Being, created from nothing and lowered down to Turtle Island. But it is also a construct that does not refer to anything. The spiritual perception asserted here only comes from a physical apprehension of reality. It is outside the scope of possibility, from a static physical perspective, for me to describe this dynamic spiritual way.

When the Anishinaabeg began their migration they took everything with them. They carried their physical possessions (which were likely not many for ease of travel) but they also brought along their spiritual understanding of reality (their bundles, scrolls, Teachings, etc.) — a wisdom which was indeed ancient and firmly rooted in the Original Instructions given to the people before they were placed on Earth. These Instructions are not codified lists of 'do's and don'ts' — they are 'the good' that is, the essence of the spirit of the people. But even 'the good' is still my static way of describing reality. There is just no other way of expressing it.

Chinshinabe

In the Anishinaabe tradition there is reference to an ancient people: the *Chinshinabe*[xiii.] The *Chinshinabe* were and are the wise people. They are the ones who trace their wisdom to the spirit of reality. They are the philosophers and the spiritual leaders. What follows is my attempt to present Anishinaabe philosophy as explained by the *Chinshinabe* tradition.

In the following pages, I endeavour to isolate what I see as three possible main components of Anishinaabe philosophy: *Kendaaswin* (knowledge), *Aazhikenimonenaadizid Bemaadizid* (the study of the way of life), and *Eyaa'oyaanh* (identity). *Kendaaswin*, because of the importance of knowledge in Anishinaabe philosophy, sets out a foundation for the remaining sections. *Aazhikenimonenaadizid Bemaadizid* is the study of the way of life that I am attempting to describe. I will examine various aspects of Anishinaabe *Mino-Bimaadiziwin* beginning with cultural stories and traditional Teachings and what living in an Anishinaabe world means. Finally, *Eyaa'oyaanh* discusses issues pertaining to a person's journey through life. It is a personal discussion of the ideal path of life and how this path is actualized through *Nwenamdanwin* (choice-making) and *N'dendowin* (personal responsibility-taking).

Notes

---

[1] Benton-Banai, The Mishomis Book, Voice of the Ojibway, 94.

[2] Ibid., 95.

[3] Ibid.

[4] For a more complete account of the Seven Fires Prophecies and the migration of the Anishinaabeg please refer to Edward-Benton-Banai, *The Mishomis Book, The Voice of the Ojibway.*

[5] See Figure 1

[6] Deloria, Jr., *God is Red*, 102.

[7] James Dumont, "Journey To Daylight-Land Through Ojibwa Eyes", in *The First Ones: Readings in Indian/Native Studies*, ed. David Miller, (Saskatchewan: Saskatchewan Indian Federated College Press, 1992), 75.

[8] Traditional Teacher, conversation with author, 1995. See Figure 2, p. 160.

[9] Bourgeois, "Odewegewin: An Ojibwe Epistemology", 49-50.

[10] Within the word *Anishinaabe* is *Anishaa* which means "nothing."

[11] Benton-Banai, *The Mishomis Book, Voice of the* Ojibway, 2.

[12] Paul Bourgeois, conversation with author, 1998.

[13] Dominic Beaudry (Odawa), conversation with author, 1998. Chinshinabe is a compound Odawa word made up of *Gchi* (great) *nishin* (good) and *abe* (being). There is a reference in this word to those beings that comprehend the Ancient Great Mystery of the 'good' way of life, of the essence of existence. Chinshinabe are the Ancient Ones, the ones from before time. In contemporary times, Chinshinabe is used to refer to the Elders of a community.

Chapter 4

Kendaaswin

Walk in Beauty on the Blessing Way.
Find your home, and when you do, you will know everything there is to know.

Traditional Native Axiom[i]

*K*endaaswin[ii] is the way of learning, the way of gathering knowledge. To understand and experience any kind of knowledge the Anishinaabeg first internalize it within their minds. They then feel the knowledge internally, through reflection, and externally, through observation. What is felt externally then becomes the objective side of learning but understanding is based on a holistic process.

It is a process of learning since knowledge is always received from outside. It is said that knowledge comes and marks one, like a mark on a birch-bark scroll.[iii] Knowledge is itself composed of the 'Teachings received'. One unveils knowledge, mental attributes and abilities as the ideal Path of Life is revealed, stage by stage, through one's active involvement in its actualization. A person also learns that truth is found within the self and not solely in the exterior world. The ability to recognize the answer is already part of a person's spirit; it is merely a process of learning to ask the right questions to unleash the potential of truth. However, learning to ask the right questions is directed by years of learning to balance emotions, listening and watching, reflection and finally, doing.[iv]

Knowledge, in western traditions, is generally thought to be located in the mind; i.e., an object of thought. The mind for the Anishinaabeg is *noodin*. This verb refers to the movement of the mind. *Noodin* is also the word that describes being windy. This is the way the mind is understood: it is blown around by the force of knowledge that acts from the exterior upon the mind (i.e., *Nenemowin*: the way of thought). It is also understood that *minjimendamowin* (the way of remembering; i.e., memory) is literally the act of holding in and stitching together that knowledge that comes to a person.[v]

It is important to remember that knowledge, for the Anishinaabeg, is singular; that is, uniform and whole. I have divided knowledge into seven aspects in order that this exploration could be carried out in a systematic manner. It can be said that these seven aspects of knowledge, as a whole, can be termed Primary Experiential Knowledge since the whole person is involved in the process of learning. With reference to the personal nature of knowledge Vine Deloria, Jr. (Sioux) explains:

> The difference between non-Western and Western knowledge is that knowledge is personal for non-Western peoples and impersonal for the Western [person]. [Western people] believe that anyone can use knowledge: for American Indians, only those people given the knowledge by other entities can use it properly.[vi]

This sense of the 'giving' of knowledge is due to the understanding that all of Creation is an interconnected reality. It may appear to us that there is separation or differentiation, as with my treatment of knowledge sources, but it is most fundamentally a harmony of unity.

With this, we will progress through a general discussion of some of the underlying epistemic sources that delineate the process of knowledge learning.

Bzindamowin (Way of Learning from Listening): Acquired Knowledge

Bzindamowin is a sort of way of coming to knowledge that develops from hearing cultural stories. This knowledge is acquired through exposure to cultural stories since they have within them implicit lessons and directives for living a good life. Pam Colorado (Oneida), in discussing the role of stories, in this case of the Teaching about relations, explains:

> The Indian theory of relatedness demands that each and every entity in the Universe seeks and sustains personal relationships. Furthermore, the spiritual aspect of knowledge about the world teaches that relationships not be left incomplete. Traditional protocols, Native language and stories teach the lesson of relations. For an example, let us look at the function of the story. Native stories, which may be 30 to 50,000 years old, have the ability to integrate and synthesize all the living relationships or events at any given moment in life. When we rely on a story to guide us we are not only integrated with the natural environment around us and with our living relations, but also with the timeless past and culture of our ancestors. Because American Indian cultures are so ancient, and the stories so old, there is almost no human experience or learning which has not been recorded in these stories. Moreover, they are tied intricately with motion, relations, and a sense of the collapsed time that there is a spiritual essence to them which people often describe as timeless.[vii]

The power of the cultural story's ability to teach comes, in part, from its repetition and its use of extraordinary and humorous situations. These cultural narratives, as explained by T. Overholt and J. Baird Callicott:

> ... convey a picture of the good life which seems at once obvious and reasonable: the "central goal of life," which the Ojibwa designate by the term pimadaziwin, [actually a Cree term, the Ojibwe is Bimaadiziwin] .... The Narratives also make it clear that man needs help

in achieving these goals. Individual competence in relationships with persons and techniques for survival is seen to depend upon the good will of other-than-human-persons.... It seems that in these narratives men are always found in the role of receivers.[viii]

For the Anishinaabeg, the telling of a cultural story has two sides. On the one side, the cultural story is told by a human being. This person is in a position whereby other people are willing to spend time with that person. This is the human aspect of the cultural narrative: the relationship between listener and cultural storyteller — engaged visually, orally and intellectually. Dennis Tedlock explains that:

> The storytellers can talk about stories, but their observations and speculations come from accumulated experience at hearing and telling stories, not from the recollection of a lesson plan.[ix]

Tedlock also adds that:

> ... the teller is not merely repeating memorized words, nor is he or she merely giving a dramatic "oral interpretation" or "concert reading" of a fixed script. We are in the presence of a performing art, all right, but we are getting the criticism at the same time and from the same person. The interpreter does not merely play the parts, but is the narrator and commentator as well.[x]

The audience sees the actions and movements of the cultural storyteller, hears the cultural storyteller's words and pays intellectual attention to the underlying meanings of those words. Mary Black-Rogers, in her forward to Overholt and Callicott's book, *Clothed-In-Fur and Other Tales: An Introduction to an Ojibwa World View*, recalls that:

> At the time I first began learning from Ojibwa Elders, "stories" just seemed to hold things up. Time and again I had to hang onto my patience through precious hours expanded on shaggy-dog accounts that often appeared to have little or no explicit relation to the subject at hand. Time and again I was told, "They used to tell stories to teach us about that." Time and again a question devised for an efficiently informative yes-or-no response elicited instead a mysteriously uninformative "story". At least one thing was clear: they were in no hurry to teach me their ways. And I was gradually learning that being explicit and being in a hurry about it are two of the cultural differences between us. The learning that takes place at this meta-level is one important yield from the story situation. ... These too take time to ingest, and especially, perhaps, they take repetition. Not exact repetition, not reduplicated unvarying sequences and personnel, but a constantly changing recombination of the elements. First the elements become familiar, then the probable and possible combinations. ... I gradually began to feel the pleasure of recognizing and anticipating, yet being freshly entertained by each novel twist, finding joy in each storyteller's innovations. For these innovations still conform to acceptable rules and patterns; they are twists that cause the listener to exclaim, "Yes, of course!"[xi]

The other side of the cultural story is found in the meaning of the Anishinaabe word for a cultural story: *aadizookaan*. *Aadizookaan* is considered a non-human person; i.e., the spirit of the story. This added dimension to the meaning of the *aadizookaan* and the *aadizookaan*'s ability to pass on knowledge directly allows a greater degree of knowledge acquisition. The *aadizookaan* speaks to the listener through the voice of the human cultural storyteller. A. Irving Hallowell captures the essence of *aadizookaan* when he explains that:

> The significant thing about these stories is that the characters in them are regarded as living entities who have existed from time immemorial. While there is a genesis through birth and temporary or permanent form-shifting through transformation, there is no outright creation. Whether human or animal in form or name, the major characters in the myth behave like people, though many of their activities are depicted in a spacio-temporal framework of cosmic, rather than mundane, dimensions. There is "social interaction" among them and between them and [the Anishinaabeg].[xii]

Aadizookaan, as a living being, has the ability to connect directly with the people who listen to the *aadizookaan*'s words. *Aadizookaan* is never static in style. There is a constant change, as in life, of the form of *aadizookaan*. Hallowell further explains that:

> A striking fact furnishes a direct linguistic cue to the attitude of the Ojibwa towards these personages. When they use the term [aadizookaan], they are not referring to what I have called a "body of narratives." The term refers to what we would call the characters in these stories; to the Ojibwa they are living persons of an-other-than-human class.[xiii]

The cultural storyteller, as the human voice of *aadizookaan* has the added ability to 'shape' the cultural story, to make it appropriate to the time and to the situation. Nevertheless, the cultural storyteller is in a spiritual union with *aadizookaan*; the message that *aadizookaan* shares, that is being expressed, remains constant through time. Hertha Dawn Wong expresses this when she explains that:

> Language for Native Americans, however, especially for pre-Columbian Native Americans, is considered sacred. To speak is not a casual affair, but a holy action. Words not only describe the world, but actively create and shape that world. ... To speak, then, is to reveal, to make manifest one's spirit. To speak one's life is to give forth the spirit of one's life, and if others join in the telling [as with aadizookaan and the storyteller] the result is a mingling of breaths, of lives, of spirits.[xiv]

A cultural story is not a socially constructed narrative since it is spiritually based. It is a dynamic teacher that helps humans achieve *Mino-Bimaadiziwin*. For the Anishinaabeg, it is understood that the *aadizookaan* tells them a story of something that actually happened in the past. Again, the past is seen in different ways. There is the human past; the history of the people and of events that took place before the present. There is also the past of non-human beings. This is not to say that there are in fact two pasts, one for humans and one for non-humans, but rather different dimensions of the same past. There is the past before the beginning of time, before the unfolding of Creation and even a past before the past before the beginning of time. All these seemingly different pasts are understood as different expressions of one past, common to all beings. Thus, as the people listen, they hear a spiritual history unique to the Anishinaabeg.

Aadizookaan is not founded on a fictional character, but a being that is beyond time, beyond the limitations of space. *Aadizookaan* has the ability to interact with the human world, observing its progress of successes and failures throughout time, and *aadizookaan* has the ability to share and reflect that knowledge with the people.

It has been said that humans must learn to centre their minds, focusing their being to hear and understand *aadizookaan* since they are normally unable to hear the words of a non-human being.[xv] The concept of 'centring one's mind' means that a person has found a profound spiritual balance of mind, body, emotion and spirit. The Anishinaabeg have the cultural storyteller, a person with a centred mind, a person able to understand and communicate the words of *aadizookaan*. This cultural storyteller, as the voice of *aadizookaan*, is able to convey these words into a form that is understandable by the people.

In some cases, *aadizookaan* can find a path into a person's dreams, and in that expanded dimension of reality, is able to communicate, in some instances, directly without the use of the uttered word.[xvi] *Aadizookaan* and the dreamer are able to share knowledge directly through the spirit. In the dream, the spoken word is replaced by the meaning, the implicit understanding of thought; in essence, it is meta-linguistic. There are also people that develop a centred mind in their waking life, and it is these people who have the ability to communicate directly with *aadizookaan*. These are the cultural storytellers of the people.

Anishinaabe Kendaaswin: Traditional Knowledge

Anishinaabe Kendaaswin as a means of attaining knowledge, although very similar to *Bzindamowin*, has the distinction of being ceremonial in nature. As I began attending seasonal ceremonies, I became aware that traditional knowledge is knowledge that is passed down from one generation to the next in ceremonial Teachings. For the Anishinaabeg, these traditional Teachings deal with philosophical Teachings. An added aspect of the ceremonial nature of the Teachings includes the use of ceremonial songs: songs sung by the singer or songs sung by non-human beings with the voice of the human singer. These sources of knowledge are directly linked to the Spirit of Creation. Ceremony acts as a process that allows for the sharing of knowledge through the voice of *Gzhe-mnidoo*. Traditional knowledge deals with the philosophy of the people; of expressing that worldview. This knowledge is shared in a way that allows for the exploration of life. Traditional knowledge defines various aspects of Creation, explaining and investigating these sacred truths. It examines the structure and purpose of *Enadizewin*, the law of Creation, of which all beings, human and non-human are a part.

Traditional knowledge is also knowledge necessary to function properly in this world. This knowledge is the basis for the proper way to prepare and carry out a hunt for example. There may be a Ceremony for a child's first hunt, with the Elders and traditional Teachers sharing their knowledge of proper behaviour. This may also entail the proper ceremonial process to ready oneself for the hunt, of asking an animal to share his/her life, of explaining the purpose of the hunt to that animal. It can be the knowledge necessary to perform a Ceremony, how to build a Sweat Lodge or an Initiation Lodge, how to be a midwife, or how to collect and prepare *Mishkikiwan* (natural medicines). This knowledge is passed down from one generation to the next in a culturally prescribed fashion. This knowledge allows a person to interact with the larger world around them. It teaches a person the interconnectedness of life and the role that humans play in this system.

Ceremonies are a time where the accumulated wisdom of the people is passed along to a new generation, thus ensuring a continuum of proper behaviour and attitude in life. Traditional knowledge, as it is passed down, gives a sense of continuity and connection with the past. There is a feeling of safety and comfort in knowing that the traditional knowledge that one learns is countless generations old. It is knowledge that finds its origin in the setting of *Enadizewin* in Creation, and it is a knowledge that gives one a direct connection with Creation.

Traditional knowledge teaches one why it is the proper time to pick a certain berry, or why the natural rice is ready to harvest. It teaches why a certain medicine should be used for a given ailment. It teaches why birch-bark should be removed from the tree in early spring so that the birch tree remains protected during the cold of winter and the heat of summer. Traditional knowledge teaches respect for all life. It fosters a relationship with all living beings, allowing one to find his or her place in the world but also allowing the necessary foundation for the examination of that world. Traditional knowledge comes from the interaction and observation of the people with their environment. Through observation of the natural world, the people learn the *Enadizewin* of Creation.

Gnawaaminjigewin (To Witness): Knowledge from Observation

Knowledge from observation also has many aspects. Initially, it can be understood as empirical knowledge: knowledge that comes from observing the world. This can be termed scientific knowledge. As a person observes the world they see the changing of the seasons — especially the characteristic features of each. By observation one learns, for example, that many animals give birth in early spring, that maple and birch sap begins to run in the spring when the days are bright with strong sunlight and the nights are cold. Observation also shows that certain berries appear and ripen at a certain time, and also when one should use snowshoes in the winter.

Observation can also be understood as the relationship between a person and the natural world. A person learns through acquired and traditional knowledge that they are intimately related with all aspects of the world. Rather than a simple 'trial and error' process of learning, the people learn by interacting directly with their environment as student with teacher. Many hunters, for example, will say that they learn a great deal from the moose they hunt every year. This is not simply learning about moose behaviour by observation, but the interaction of the moose and the man as relatives. By learning the traditional process of preparation for a moose hunt, the hunter centres his being so that he is able to communicate with the moose directly. As Hallowell explains:

> Speaking as an Ojibwa, one might say: all other persons — human and other-than-human — are structured the same as I am. There is a vital part which is enduring and an outward appearance that may be transformed under certain conditions. All other "persons," too, have such attributes as self-awareness and understanding. I can talk with them. Like myself, they have personal identity, autonomy, and volition. I cannot always predict exactly how they will act, although most of the time their behavior meets my expectations. In relation to myself, other "persons" vary in power. Many have more power that I have, but some have less.[xvii]

Traditional knowledge teaches that one must ask the moose to share his or her life. When this process is carried out properly, the moose that has offered him or herself will allow the hunter to make the kill. But the act of hunting is more that the killing of an animal, it is a learning experience whereby the moose will teach the hunter about moose behaviour. But this is not only by physical observation; the hunter will learn the proper calls, when to stand down-wind, when to rub himself with moose urine, etc. through a direct spiritual interaction with the moose. The moose teaches the hunter the proper way to hunt and kill so that there is a minimal amount of suffering. The moose will lead the hunter through the woods, revealing trails and wallows. The moose teaches the hunter the patience and stealth necessary for a good hunt. The moose is a relative in Creation and thus deserves familial respect. Vine Deloria, Jr. (Sioux) explains this well when he states that:

> Here, power and place are dominant concepts — power being the living energy that inhabits and/or composes the universe, and place being the relationship of things to each other ... put into a simple equation: power and place produce personality. This equation simply means that the universe is alive, but it also contains within it the very important suggestions that the universe is personal and, therefore, must be approached in a personal manner ... The personal nature of the universe demands that each and every entity in it seek and sustain personal relationships. Here, the Indian theory of relativity is much more comprehensive than the corresponding theory articulated by Einstein and his fellow scientists. The broader Indian idea of relationship, in a universe very

personal and particular, suggests that all relationships have a moral content. For that reason, Indian knowledge of the universe was never separated from other sacred knowledge about ultimate spiritual realities. The spiritual aspect of knowledge about the world taught the people that relationships must not be left incomplete. There are many stories about how the world came to be, and the common themes running through them are the completion of relationships and the determination of how this world should function.[xviii]

The traditional hunter hunts for survival, recognizing the moose as a giver of life: one of the moose's roles in Creation. The traditional hunter also recognizes the moose as a teacher and guide, and not as a prize or a trophy. There is no joy in the hunt. The hunter is taking a life, and this choice is coupled with the responsibility of hunting in a good way. There is not the sadistic joy of 'killing for the sake of killing' as in sport hunting. There is the sense that killing is something which is done in the sense of ultimate necessity — for survival and life. There is in fact great 'joy' in killing the moose, but it is the joy of life and living. I see hunting as a necessary part of life. It is a great reminder of and an essential communion with life. In essence, killing with the proper intentions is a re-affirmation and recognition of life.

Knowledge through observation also includes the study of animals and plants and their relationship with the natural world. By observation one learns, for example, the power of Fasting from the bear, the purifying nature of maple and birch sap, the healing properties of new cedar shoots, the process of damming from the beaver. Knowledge from observation coupled with acquired and traditional knowledge allows a person to live in harmony with the world.

Manidoo-waabiwin (Seeing in a Spirit Way):
Revealed Knowledge

Revealed knowledge is that knowledge gained through events that are considered spiritual. These events may be dreams, visions, or intuition. In all of these cases, a person finds him/herself in direct communication with the Spirit. There is an interaction between person and spirit that transcends one's physical reality.

Dreams[xix]

In the case of dreams, a person is in a state of awareness that allows them to go beyond the limits of the physical. Overholt and Callicott explain that:

> Every society has a complicated set of mechanisms for passing on its world view, and in traditional Ojibwa culture the telling of the myths and stories was an important part of this process. Of course, these narratives did not have to bear the entire burden of transmitting the world view. Dreams were also important, so much so that one could speak of children going "to school in dreams," ...[xx]

From my personal experience I have realized that there are two main kinds of dreams: lucid and non-lucid. Each has its role to play in revealing spiritual knowledge. Non-lucid dreams are dreams where the dreamer is not aware that they are dreaming.

Nevertheless, non-lucid dreams are always meaningful. They are sources of knowledge that come to the dreamer directly.

Lucid dreams are those dreams where the dreamer is aware that they are dreaming. Being aware, the dreamer is able to interact within the dream environment. Lucid dreams can also be further subdivided into two classes; namely, active and non-active. Physically active dreams are those where a person is able to move in sleep (generally referred to as 'sleep-walking'). These dreams usually present themselves as a combination of the physical waking world and the dream world. A person is able to move about in her/his physical environment with the added dimension of the dream environment superimposed upon the physical. This kind of dream reveals the full dimension of the world. The dreamer is both asleep and awake at the same time. This dream experience can manifest itself, for example, as human and non-human dream people present in one's bedroom. It can also manifest itself as a voyage that the dreamer takes. The dreamer is able to leave her/his sleeping environment and travel to other places. These places may also exist in the physical realm and the dreamer is able to travel great distances.

The dreamer is able to communicate directly with the beings in his/her dream, sometimes using the spoken word and other times through the sharing of thought directly. It is even possible for a person in this dream state to communicate with people who are in the waking physical state. Hallowell explains that:

> The basic assumption that links [other-than-human-persons] with dreams is this: Self-related experience of the most personal and vital kind includes what is seen, heard, and felt in dreams. Although there is no lack of discrimination between the experiences of the self when awake and when dreaming, both sets of experiences are equally self-related. Dream experiences function integrally with other self-recalled memory images in so far as these, too, enter the field of self-awareness. When we [i.e., non-Natives] think autobiographically we only include events that happened to us awake; the Ojibwa include remembered events that have occurred in dreams. And, far from being of subordinate importance, such experiences are for them often of more vital importance than the events of daily waking life. Why is this so? Because it is in dreams that the individual comes into direct communication with the [other-than-human-person], the powerful person of the other-than-human class.[xxi]

The dreamer may 'talk', for example, with a bear or a porcupine directly as I have in my dreams. The ancestors of the dreamer may appear in a dream to share their knowledge of the past. Questions can be answered, and physical-spiritual contact can be made.

Naanaagede'enmowin (Visions)

Visions are evidence of how a person is able to interact with the spirit world. During a Ceremony such as the Sweat Lodge, the spirits of the four directions as well as the spirits of the Grandfathers and Grandmothers are invited into the Sweat Lodge. They enter to hear the people, but also to respond to them. As a person finds balance in the Sweat Lodge, it is possible to hear the voice of the Spirit. Again it is not a voice limited to the spoken word, it is a voice that can also enter the mind and the spirit. And it is also possible to see and touch the Spirit; to visualize the source of the knowledge as it is shared. There are times when a person is unable to find the balance necessary to interact directly with the Spirit, but there is always a conductor in the Sweat Lodge who has attained a level of spiritual balance that allows him or her to communicate and relay the message of the Spirit to that person.

It is also possible to interact directly with the Spirit during *Makadekewin*, (the Fast), although there are visions attained in other ways. The Faster prepares him or herself by abstaining from food and water for a certain amount of time. As the Faster gets past the thirst and hunger, the loneliness, fear and anger, he or she leaves the physical realm, elevated to the higher place, becoming a pure non-physical spirit. In this way the Faster is able to communicate directly with those of the spirit world. Fasting is quiet meditation based on the lack of physical distractions. This is different than the dream, where a person is still intimately attached to her/his physical self. During the Fast, a person is separated from her/his physical self and is able to go beyond physical space and time. The vision is an event of great spiritual importance. It is a directive for a person's life. It functions as a way for the person to find the purpose of her/his life.

Vision can provide a person with one's name, one's Clan and even the meaning of one's life, to name a few gifts. During a vision, a person may be able to meet his/her spirit helpers: teachers that will guide a person throughout one's life. The vision can indicate and even direct a person to her/his life purpose. In essence, the vision is the process of self-discovery; a person's true identity is revealed to her/him. In a dream, a person is given Teachings that allow one the knowledge necessary for a good life, but a vision also reveals one's spirit, one's identity as having a good purpose and place in Creation. A vision sets the very foundation of life, while dreams and other sources of knowledge set out how one should live that life. Ultimately, the vision allows a person to interact directly with all of Creation.

Gidisi'ewin (Intuition)

Intuition is the sudden awareness of understanding. It is sometimes described as a feeling, or a hunch. However, intuition is more than a feeling; it is a direct understanding that comes from a well-balanced life. This kind of knowledge is also spiritual since a person has a complete spirit identity. Knowledge is always received from the exterior; through acquisition, tradition, observation and revelation; but, intuition, as a form of revealed knowledge, points to a built-in truth recognition. In other words, truth or the ability to perceive truth is the 'feeling' that one has, at the moment of intuitive clarity. Intuition is the voice of one's spirit — the spirit that received *Gzhe-mnidoo's* instructions before it came to this Earth. Our respective intuition speaks to each of us about what we are doing, or not doing, while we are here. Whether this clarity comes when faced with a decision or one's attempts to understand the meaning of a cultural story or traditional teaching, there is a clear understanding of being 'right' about a thought or decision. This intuitive sort of knowledge, based on external knowledge sources, is the outcome of a balanced person able to think and feel in a balanced way; of being able to centre one's mind. All knowledge is found in Creation, but the ability to understand with clarity lies within each individual.

Kiimiingona manda Kendaaswin [xxii] *(Instructions from Gzhe-mnidoo): Original Instructions*

It is taught that the Anishinaabeg were given Seven Gifts from the Seven Grandfathers of the Star World. These Seven Gifts include wisdom, love, respect, bravery, honesty, humility and truth, which may be defined in the following way:

> To cherish knowledge is to know wisdom
>
> To know love is to know peace
>
> To honor all of Creation is to have respect
>
> Bravery is to face the foe with integrity
>
> Honesty in facing a situation is to be brave
>
> Humility is to know yourself as a sacred part of Creation
>
> Truth is to know all of these things [xxiii]

These Seven Gifts begin and end with knowledge and the ability to know. This is the beginning and end of being a good person. Life becomes 'something-lived' based on reflection. Thought is defined as a union of mind and intuition (Couture's full-mindedness). It is said that one must centre one's mind in order to apprehend and understand Creation. One can turn one's mind back to the beginning, and even before the beginning of time.

As the Seven Grandfathers have taught, to cherish knowledge is to know wisdom. This is the first step in a philosophical apprehension of existence. Knowledge is the means to being a good person. This tradition stresses the need to investigate the world, and as such it is taught that philosophical thought has conceptual and logical beauty. This realization unleashes one's imagination and liberates one's thinking. The domain of thought/intuition opens up an infinity of possibilities. Individuals are choice-makers, and they are also thought-makers. They are able to grasp the import of *Nwenamdanwin* (choice-making), to ascertain the underlying why of Creation and not only the how (or what) of Creation. Like *Gzhe-mnidoo* who, at the beginning of Creation, sent out thoughts to see if there was anything or anyone else[xxiv], the individual also sends out one's thoughts to learn about one's world through Teachings received.

The Seven Gifts — wisdom, love, respect, bravery, honesty, humility and truth — are all dependent on knowledge since being good means knowing all these things: it is important to live these gifts, choosing to actualize their potentiality. These Seven Gifts give us a way of knowing *Mino-Bimaadiziwin* in its fullest sense. Nevertheless, they are not the Original Instructions of *Gzhe-mnidoo*. They are gifts that help us live this life.

The Original Instructions are not really instructions such as the Christian Ten Commandments, for instance. The instructions are, for lack of a better expression, encoded in our being, our spirit. The Anishinaabeg are inherently the Good Beings. The directive from *Gzhe-mnidoo* is very simple: be good. The actualization of this directive is, on the other hand, very difficult: the very challenge of life.

Eshkakimikwe-Kendaaswin: Mother-Earth Knowledge

Eshkakimikwe is Mother to all life: mineral beings, plant beings, animal and insect beings and, lastly, human beings. She is both the source of life as well as its unconditional nurturer.

Gidisi'ewin means the navel way. It is the Mother connection. In the same way that my physical body was connected to my mother through my navel, my spirit is connected to *Eshkakimikwe* through my spirit navel. But unlike the fact that my umbilical chord was cut at birth, my spiritual connection to *Eshkakimikwe* can never be severed.

The presence and *Zaagedewin* (love) of *Eshkakimikwe* is an underlying constant. *Eshkakimikwe* unfolds beneath our feet as the actual and symbolic ground on which we stand. Without Mother there would be no life and no reason to live. This may seem mystical in context, but mystical or not it is the very truth by which we exist. All life feels a tie to Earth Mother. The one fact that seems to distinguish Aboriginal peoples from their western relations is that Aboriginal cultures understand that the umbilical cord was never cut. Like a foetus in her/his mother, each of us is constantly drawing physical and spiritual nutrition from our Earth Mother. We cannot go anywhere without her, and even in our most far-reaching voyages we are dependent on the nutrition our Mother creates for us; any astronaut would attest to this.

So what is it about Earth Mother that permeates Anishinaabe philosophy? In a word: circularity. We are witnesses to the circularity of the seasons, of life and death and life again, and of all the other cycles that drive our very existence. This is the way of life.

Manidoo-minjimendamowin (Spirit Memory): Spirit Identity

Physical life begins at conception. The union of a mother's and father's physical essence combines to create a physical body. At conception one's spirit joins with the physical body to create the whole person. Even though the spirit is not defined by space-time, the union is one that exists over time.

The spirit that fuses with the physical body carries with it the identity of that person. Since this spirit is beyond the constraints of space-time, identity is eternal. I remember my earliest awareness of this fact. As I previously explained, I am of mixed heritage; nevertheless, my experience the first time I heard the drum as well as the first time I attended ceremonies was an awakening of my Anishinaabe spirit. This was explained to me as 'blood memory' or 'spirit memory'. Paul Bourgeois (Ojibwe) states:

> Some Elders have talked about this type of [identity] experience as stemming from "blood memory" and scientists are beginning to view it as "genetic memory." I am calling the experience as based in our "spirit memory." This spirit memory, I believe, is something we as human beings have, but is perhaps something we have lost and forgotten through disuse and separation from the primacy of human experience.[xxv]

This spirit memory is something that transcends time and space. It is said that all the experiences of my ancestors can be revealed to me throughout my life. Part of my responsibility in physical life is to 'remember' this knowledge. It is also my responsibility to add to this body of knowledge so that it can be passed on to my descendants.

Stages of Knowledge Learning

This brings us to the organization of knowledge as set out in four stages: feeling, watching, reflection and doing. The explanation of these stages in the learning of knowledge will become clearer in light of the above discussion.

Feeling

Feeling refers to a state of balanced emotions, once one realizes that one is completely responsible for all choices. This emotional balance is the most difficult task that one faces in life. The Elders teach that emotional balance — through trusting one's intuition *and* one's reason — allows one to hear and see with open ears, clear eyes and a good heart.

Watching and Listening

Watching and listening is a vital aspect of knowledge since one is able to learn many things without asking questions; i.e., experiential learning. At times, asking too many questions obscures the obvious knowledge available in the physical-spiritual world. Observation without questioning also teaches patience and humility since one is forced to quiet one's natural inclination to want to know everything all at once. A person learns in a gradual way, coming to understand that all things come at their own pace and that forcing answers has a way of moving one further away from one's goal. In this way one also gains knowledge about one's own self and finds balance in one's emotional self.

Reflection

With balanced emotions and having watched and listened patiently, one ultimately arrives at the time of thinking and reflection. It is here that one uses the power of one's mind and spirit to reflect upon the knowledge that one has gained, understanding it for what it means, and for what it can do in one's life. A person is able to reflect on the process as well, of balancing one's emotions, of watching and listening and finding knowledge about one's behaviour and attitudes. Knowledge is a constant companion. It is one's duty in life to make its acquaintance so that one can receive wisdom and find one's own truth within one's self.

Doing

It is after careful reflection that one is ready to do something. It may be the first time that one is asked to help in the Lodge; i.e., singing or even being asked to give one of the Teachings. Whatever the task may be, one is able to do it with confidence and courage since one has spent time readying oneself for the moment (although from personal experience I never really felt ready the first time, still afraid of making mistakes). It is also important to understand that anything that may be left out or done in error will be corrected by an Elder or Teacher, thus affording a continuation of one's learning. For many this is the most difficult aspect of experiential learning since there can be feelings of guilt, frustration, anger or disappointment when corrected. It takes a great deal of confidence to overcome these feelings, and to again strive for balanced emotions. The learning process is always inclusive though, and any corrections are made without any intention of personal criticism. Couture (Cree/Métis) explains that:

> The Elders apply a learning-by-doing model, counseling and teaching focus on the doing, on one's experience. Respectful observation eventually yields evidence of remarkable, incisive intellect, of tested wisdom, of sharp and comprehensive observational ability allied with excellent memory recall, and of well developed discursive ability — abilities and skills which constitute the main cognitive qualities of an Elders' mind.[xxvi]

Usually, a teacher will add the parts that were missed or mistakenly added after the apprentice has finished speaking, or a process will be redone by the teacher. There is never a direct confrontational exchange, only the uncritical addition and correction within the context of the event. Errors and omissions are part of an apprentice's life, and they are reminded to learn from one's accomplishments as well as one's errors.

The time of doing is also a time of question-asking; for clarification, for direction, or for a new Teaching. The process of asking questions is such that one feels the right time to ask a teacher. Of course this teacher may be human, but also non-human. Again, one never rushes into questioning until one has learned from watching and listening first.

Manidookewin (Ceremony)

These four stages of knowledge are all brought together in Ceremony. Ceremony allows one to cross the seeming divide between physical and spiritual realms, whereby one can observe with a more complete perception. The Anishinaabeg are empiricists of sorts, going out into the world searching for knowledge. Moreover, the Anishinaabeg have the ability to search in dimensions that exceed that of the physical.

The Fast is an example of how the four stages of knowledge are applied. During my Fasting experiences I have found that there must be a balance of emotional, mental, spiritual and physical states to go without water and food for a number of days. My time in the Fasting Lodge is spent sleeping as much as possible and always watching and listening when awake and in sleep. There is also a great deal of thinking and reflection during this time alone; dealing with myself and why I am there, as well as what I am learning. Finally, the doing comprises the actual Fast and the time after, specifically during the Coming-out Ceremony, when one may choose to speak about some of the experiences in the Fasting Lodge. The process of coming to knowledge learning entails a balancing of all the aspects of one's life: mind, body, emotion, and spirit. It is a journey in the actualization of a good life.

Notes

[1] Couture, "Native Studies and the Academy", 4.

[2] I must acknowledge Dr. Marlene Brant Castellano's work in the area of Aboriginal knowledge. Dr. Brant Castellano, a Mohawk woman, has begun a general discussion concerning many of the points on which I elaborate here. (see Marlene Brant Castellano, "Updating Aboriginal Traditions of Knowledge" in *Indigenous Knowledge: Multiple Readings of Our World* (Toronto: University of Toronto Press, forthcoming, 1998), (used with her kind permission).

[3] Traditional Teacher, conversation with author, 1996.

[4] Ibid.

[5] Ibid.

[6] Deloria, Jr., *Red Earth, White Lies*, 53.

[7] Pam Colorado, "Bridging Native and Western Science," *Convergence* XXI (2/3) 49-67, Toronto, ON: International Council for Adult Education, 1988: 55.

[8] T. Overholt and J. Baird Callicott, *Clothed-In-Fur and Other Tales: An Introduction to an Ojibwa World View* (Lanham, MD: University Press of America, 1982), 115.

[9] Dennis Tedlock and Barbara Tedlock, (eds.), *Teachings from the American Earth* (New York: Liveright, 1975), 15.

[10] Ibid., 236.

[11] Mary Black-Rogers, forward to *Clothed-In-Fur and Other Tales: An Introduction to an Ojibwa World View* by T. Overholt and J. Baird Callicott (Lanham, MD: University Press of America, 1982), xv-xvi.

[12] A. Irving Hallowell, "Ojibwa Ontology, Behavior, and World View" in *Teachings from the American Earth* by Dennis Tedlock and Barbara Tedlock, (eds.) (New York: Liveright, 1975), 150.

[13] Ibid.

[14] Hertha Dawn Wong, *Sending My Heart Back Across the Years, Tradition and Innovation in Native American Autobiography* (New York: Oxford University Press, 1992), 19.

[15] Elder, conversation with author, 1996.

[16] Personal dream experiences.

[17] Hallowell, "Ojibwa Ontology, Behavior, and World View", 168.

[18] Vine Deloria, Jr., "American Indian Metaphysics" in *Winds of Change* (Boulder, Colorado: American Indian Science and Engineering Society, June, 1986), quoted in Pam Colorado, "Bridging Native and Western Science." *Convergence* XXI (2/3): 49-67, Toronto, ON: International Council for Adult Education, 1988. 51-52.

[19] Discussion based on personal experience.

[20] T. Overholt and J. Baird Callicott, *Clothed-In-Fur and Other Tales: An Introduction to an Ojibwa World View*, 139.

[21] Hallowell, "Ojibwa Ontology, Behavior, and World View", 165.

[22] Florence Osawamick, 1997.

[23] Benton-Banai, *The Mishomis Book, Voice of the Ojibway*, 64. (emphasis added)

[24] Ibid., 2.

[25] Bourgeois, "Odewegewin: An Ojibwe Epistemology", 47.

[26] Couture, "Next Time, Try an Elder!", 13.

Chapter 5

Aazhikenimonenaadizid Bemaadizid

It is intuitively obvious to the most casual of observers.

Dr. Robert W. Malone

*A*azhikenimonenaadizid *Bemaadizid* literally means the study of the behaviour of life. It is the closest term that exists in Anishinaabemowin for the English word philosophy.[i] There is no term for philosophy *per se* in Anishinaabemowin. The word philosophy comes to us from the Greek tradition. It literally means the intellectual love of wisdom. For the Anishinaabeg, 'life' is central rather than knowledge or wisdom. Knowledge is a step towards *Mino-Bimaadiziwin* rather than the result of a good life. The Anishinaabe language does not make distinctions of something being a philosophy, or even a religion, but there is a sense of philosophical thought and religious faith. This is not to say that there is no philosophy or religion, only that there is no separation made between various aspects of Creation. Essentially, everything in Anishinaabe life is rooted in the process of life, thus *Mino-Bimaadiziwin* is of paramount importance.

Mino-Bimaadiziwin literally means the Way of a Good Life.[ii] It is a simple expression, but it contains the ontological, ethical, epistemological and aesthetic directives of life. In essence, *Mino-Bimaadiziwin* represents all the Teachings that pertain to living a long healthy life. Although it is prescriptive in nature, it allows for the freedom of choice that each individual expresses.

The Way of a Good Life must be set out for human beings. It is said that we are the last and weakest on Earth. We were placed here by *Gzhe-mnidoo* after the rest of the world, after all the minerals, plants, insects and animals had found their home. As human beings, we must struggle due to our weakened state of existence. We are dependent on others for our well-being. We depend, for example, on the mineral beings for our stone and metal, on the plant beings and the animal beings for our food and clothing. These natural beings are connected with Creation in a different way than human beings. They live with the Original Instructions as set out by Creator. Human beings, on the other hand, have the habit of ignoring or forgetting the Original Instructions. Chief Benton-Banai (Ojibwe) explains what happened to the First People of Earth when they moved away from the Original Instructions:

> I regret to say that this harmonious way of life on Earth did not last forever. Men and women did not continue to give each other the respect needed to keep the Sacred Hoop of marriage strong. Families began to quarrel with each other. Finally villages were arguing back and forth. People began to fight over hunting grounds. Brother turned against brother and began killing each other.
>
> It greatly saddened the Creator, Gitchie Manito, to see the Earth's people turn to evil ways. It seemed that the entire Creation functioned in harmony except for the people who were the last to be placed there. For a long time Gitchie Manito waited hoping that the evil ways would cease and that brotherhood, sisterhood, and respect for all things would again come to rule over the people.
>
> When it seemed that there was no hope left, Gitchie Manito decided to purify the Earth. He would do this with water. The water came like a mush-ko'-be-wun' (flood) upon the Earth. The flood came so fast that it caught the entire Creation off guard. Most all living things were drowned immediately, but some of the animals were able to keep swimming, trying to find a small bit of land on which to rest. Some of the birds were caught in the air and had to keep flying in order to stay alive.
>
> The purification of the Earth with water appeared to be complete. All the evil that had built up in the hearts of the first people had been washed away.[iii]

This purification led to the Second People of Earth.[iv]

> The second people of the Earth grew in number and their villages began to spread across the land. But, in their early years, the second people had a very hard time. At first, they were a weak people. Diseases took many lives each year. There were many times when people would be killed by just stumbling and falling down.[v]

Gradually, the new people learned of ceremonies and a way of life that allowed them to find balance and harmony with the world. This is who we are today, although many people in this world have forgotten the balance and harmony necessary to live a good life.

At the centre of *Mino-Bimaadiziwin* is a spiritual apprehension of the world and the understanding that we are related to all beings. It is this central tenet of Anishinaabe philosophy that we will now examine.

Cultural Stories and Traditional Teachings

Spirituality is the beginning of any attempt to understand Anishinaabe worldview, but it is also spirituality that is found when we finish searching for the truth. Spirituality is the underlying truth; without it our cultural codes would have been destroyed long ago, and yet they can still be found in the cultural stories and Teachings of the people.

As a mainly oral system, Anishinaabe philosophy finds its foundation and places all its merit on the truth expressed by cultural stories and traditional Teachings. James Dumont (Ojibwe) stresses that:

If we try to understand and sensibly appreciate Native myth and legend we must be willing, first of all, to accept that there is involved here a very special way of 'seeing the world'. Secondly, and a necessary further step, we must make an attempt to 'participate' in this way of seeing.[vi]

To comprehend the sense of simultaneous realities that is expressed in Anishinaabe philosophy it is imperative that any interpretation of Anishinaabe cultural stories and Teachings include a comprehensive understanding of the people themselves. The name of the people: *Anishinaabe*, means "the good being, created from nothing and lowered down to Mother Earth." Within this one word, we find our Creation Story, our purpose and our identity. Cultural stories and traditional Teachings, such as the Creation Story, elaborate on and explain what it is to be an Anishinaabe person. Cultural stories not only direct personality, social order, action and ethics; they also set out the proper context for a person's life. Cultural stories and traditional Teachings give life structure and meaning. Without these Teachers, how else can a person know how to be good? They are oral reference libraries that account for stories, legends, prophecies, ceremonies, songs, dances, language and the philosophy of the people. Moreover, the Elders and traditional Teachers responsible for these oral libraries, are as much the librarians as the libraries of this knowledge.[vii] Cultural stories and Teachings are as alive as the person hearing them or sharing them. They exist in a dynamic form and their meaning is eternal. It is for this reason that cultural stories and traditional Teachings are important, and it is for the same reason that we must listen to their voices.

What It Means To Live In an Anishinaabe World

Belief in the supernatural, transcendent and/or incorporeal side of reality is a natural aspect of Anishinaabe culture. This can be understood, on the surface, as a belief in magic and mysticism. The Spiritual world is, by definition, the opposite of objectivity and quantification. It is a realm of reality that subscribes to dynamism, movement and quality. Moreover, magic and mysticism are not simply illusions, tricks and slight-of-hand, but expressions of the mystery of Creation.

There are a number of philosophical assumptions at play here. Foremost is an acceptance of Creation as a physical-spiritual reality. It is not possible to speak of one aspect without the other. The unity of Creation is a given. The role of spiritual existence and spiritual beings is nevertheless central. As I have stated before, all life is related spiritually, and this relationship defines each being as a member of one family. In addition, like any family, each member plays various roles.[viii]

Anishinaabe as Practitioner of Mino-Bimaadiziwin

Anishinaabe philosophy is not a purely intellectual pursuit; it is a lived philosophy, a philosophy of process — a way of life. It finds meaning in the lived experience of each being of Creation and it is expressed by the concept of harmony and balance of the four aspects of life; namely, the physical, mental, emotional and spiritual.[ix] These four aspects find their place as artificial divisions of the interconnectivity of life in the Teachings expressed by the Elders and the traditional Teachers. These Teachings are static patterns in themselves but point to the dynamic unfolding of Creation.

Fundamental to this system is an inherent understanding that all life is related, and that life is a process of learning. Underlying any discussion of this worldview is the acceptance that we, as human beings, are not separate and distinct from the 'stuff' of reality. Human Beings are only one aspect of the whole.

It can be said that the Anishinaabe person is a practitioner of sorts, a practitioner of *Mino-Bimaadiziwin*. In essence, it means living life in a sacred manner due to the sacred nature of Creation. Because of the intellectual and spiritual depth with which the Anishinaabeg approach life, some of them attain the role of doctors of philosophy; i.e., traditional female and male Teachers and Elders (*Chinshinabeg*) concerned with the mental, physical, emotional and spiritual health of others. This understanding of lived-health focuses on the prevention of disease and living life to the fullest, actualizing the potentiality inherent in Creation as well as the treatment of illness.[x] There is a fine balance or equilibrium that must be achieved due to each being's responsibility in maintaining the goodness and beauty of Creation. To understand *Mino-*

Bimaadiziwin it is necessary to comprehend the importance of this responsibility.

Unity and Dignity

The singular force of Anishinaabe *Mino-Bimaadiziwin* is the idea of the unity and dignity of all beings. Rémi Savard states that:

> The genuine American dimension, to which present day Indigenous peoples urge us towards, is neither English, neither French, neither Indian, nor Inuit; it is found in the Indigenous notion of the Great Circle, in accordance with which the absolute respect of the specificity of each link becomes the indispensable condition in maintaining the whole.[xi]

Each being is an integral aspect of Creation. The Anishinaabe person, when praying, addresses his or her salutations to all beings of the universe. This allows one to recognize one's place in Creation. There is an absolute certainty of coming from somewhere. This reality is not born of some random ordering of cosmic dust, but rather the expression of *Gzhe-mnidoo*'s will. This is the underlying spiritual code of Creation as unity that maintains and gives meaning to life and how we live.

Creation as Unity

It is important here to understand fully the meaning of unity. Creation is not a movement towards unity, but rather is unity in movement. To think that Creation can only be grasped by the physical senses, or conversely, that it can only be grasped by the rational intellect, is to give either the sensible or the intellectual more importance. Creation is harmony in seeming duality. It is the unity of Being rather than the unity of the intellectual and the sensible or of the objective and the subjective. This underlying harmony is what gives meaning to the perceived dualities of life. Nevertheless, any attempt to call Creation the synthesis of this or any duality is an attempt to do away with duality. Duality is a matter of fact. Duality is found in all aspects of our lives; e.g., hot and cold, light and dark, etc. This duality is of the actual kind as experienced in life, but which can be understood only against the backdrop of Creation.

Ultimately, Creation cannot be thought of as global or creator oriented, as in a synthesis, since it is the harmony of all duality. In other words, Creation is not simply a conglomeration of all that exists (known and unknown) put together objectively by *Gzhe-mnidoo*, but it is the harmony that is found in both the total collection of all that is, and the individual beings themselves, including *Gzhe-mnidoo*. By this, I mean to say that each individual (human and non-human) is as much a representation and manifestation of the whole of Creation as the whole of Creation is a representation of itself. This may all seem rather esoteric and cryptic, but simply put it is taught that each individual is the physical-spiritual manifestation of the whole of Creation and that it is one's responsibility and duty to be good so that Creation is maintained.[xii] Creation is, and as such all that is, is Creation. For the Anishinaabeg, this understanding is the highest expression of being a good person.

To further this understanding of representation and manifestation, the Elders teach that each individual is complete at birth, and the task of life is to actualize each aspect of the potential person. Such potential includes seeking out, for instance, the meaning inherent in a person's name, one's Clan, one's special abilities, and one's role in life. At a young age, a person is taught the ability of choice-making as she/he listens to the telling of cultural stories and traditional Teachings which, in turn, actualize the listener's potential as choice-maker.

This leads us to the special way of seeing mentioned by James Dumont (Ojibwe) (1992) which entails a primacy of perception, although this is a physical-spiritual perception that transcends space-time. Humans are physical-spiritual beings that find meaning in a physical-spiritual existence. As we have seen, this philosophy is centred in Creation and all it entails. All things are interconnected; one's place in Creation brings balance and belonging in the world. Nevertheless, since one interacts with the world in a mainly physical way, it is very difficult to see the physical-spiritual unity of Creation. The Anishinaabeg overcome this difficulty as a dream conscious people who understand that dreams and visions are a doorway into the more expanded dimension of actual reality. James Dumont (Ojibwe) sums up this point when he explains that:

> There seems to be a vital link, then, for the Ojibwa, between mythical times and the present. In fact, it might be said that mythical times become present when we approach the realm of the sacred through the dream of the vision quest. Perhaps this can be expressed as simultaneous realities. What we have called mythical time is eternally present, and it occurs simultaneously with our present.[xiii]

Since Creation is a complex reality of many aspects, it is necessary to develop the proper senses to be able to 'perceive' it completely. The Anishinaabeg use Fasts or Vision Quests, the Sweat Lodge Ceremony and dreams, for instance, to expand their perception of reality. The simultaneous realities that Dumont mentions are in fact the unity in the movement of the physicality-spirituality of Creation. There becomes more to reality than simply the physical, spatial and temporal waking world. One's reality is made up of both waking and dreaming. One is aware of one's reality and part of it all the time. One is not unconscious in sleep, but in a state of learning.

By choosing to learn how to perceive the simultaneity of reality, one gradually attains a state through which the interconnectivity of Creation may be perceived.

Animism and the Actualization of Life

The Anishinaabeg are a theosophical people; that is, a people who are concerned with philosophical and spiritual thought based on a mystical insight into the divine nature of reality. Generally, terms such as 'animism' or 'pantheism' are used to describe the worldview of the Anishinaabe. This is based, I would guess, on the fact that the field of Anthropology has defined the Anishinaabeg as a people who believe that everything is alive.

I have struggled somewhat with the concept of animism, and I have always felt that it did not exactly capture the actual understanding that was taking place. I became acutely aware of this the first time I went out with a friend to gather rocks for a Sweat Lodge Ceremony.

We went into a field covered with rocks of varying sizes. We were, I was told, to look for medium sized red granite rocks. You would think that such a search would be simple. Well there we were standing for half-an-hour looking up and down that field and we could not find a single red granite rock. And then my friend took out his *asemaa* pouch saying that we needed some help. He held the *asemaa* and addressed the rocks asking them to awaken and show themselves to us. He went on to explain aloud that we needed them for our Sweat Lodge and that we would care for them well. And you know, after he put the *asemaa* down they seemed to pop out of the background of the field. They were always there, but they were now showing themselves.

The *asiniig* (rocks that have shown themselves) because of their great age are different than human beings in that they perceive time's passage, from our perspective, in a highly accelerated way. They have existed on Earth for millions of years and thus we must ask them to show themselves: in essence slow down to our temporal perception.

What does all this mean? For me, I have come to understand it as an actualization of life. This is reflected in a story that has been told so many times that it can now, I would venture to say, be called a contemporary Teaching. An Elder was asked, with regards to the question of animism, if rocks were alive. He replied "No, but some are." I have heard this story told many times during the preparation of the Sweat Lodge. I have come to understand the search for rocks for the Sweat Lodge as a process of actualizing life. A rock is just a rock, but when they are used during a *Manidookewin* (Ceremony) they become *Mishoomisag* (Grandfathers) and *Nookomisag* (Grandmothers). In so many words, they become alive. This is also true of *dewe'ganag* (drums), *zhiishiigwanag* (shakers) and other sacred objects. Outside of *Manidookewin* they are just rocks, wooden vessels and gourds. But during *Manidookewin* they are alive with all the qualities of sentience usually attributed to humans. This is not to say that these *asiniig*, *dewe'ganag* and *zhiishiigwanag* experience a radical shift from in-animation to animation at the whim of a human being, in other words a social and conceptual construct created by human minds, but rather that they are actually alive. The radical shift happens for the people who take part in the Ceremony. Ceremony is one of many occasions when humans become in-tune to the spiritual aspect of Creation; thus they are able to 'perceive' sacred objects as the actual living beings that they are.

Animism is the belief that natural objects, natural phenomena, and the universe possess spirit. In a sense, this is the way the Anishinaabeg see the world. But it is also true that the unity of Creation is a oneness. To tell you the truth, this leads me to think that what we physically perceive as a differentiated substantiality may be an illusion, but I cannot be sure. I am led to this hypothetical conclusion in part because of the Teachings that explain that Creation is a unity: that all beings are related. But more so because of the ethical prescription that each individual, as a physical manifestation of the spiritual essence of *Gzhe-mnidoo*, must strive to live a good life in order that the integrity and unity of Creation is maintained.

My experience during *Makadekewin* and many Sweat Lodge Ceremonies has revealed to me a sense of disappearing into nothingness, an existential emptiness. When I sit in a Sweat Lodge particularly, I experience a sense of expansion. Generally, a Sweat Lodge is only four or five feet tall, but sitting in that hot and moist darkness I have a sense that the Lodge expands and me with it. I can best describe it as sitting in the whole of the universe. Initially, I feel gigantic; but after a while, I loose any perspective of space and time. It is a peculiar feeling to exit the Lodge and 'return' in a sense to the realm of space-time. Whatever the truth, I want to be clear in my intentions here, I state no actual conclusion or theory, only speculation. I have reached the limit of my knowledge in this area.

Dynamic and Static

The above discussion of the physical and spiritual leads me to the central subject of this chapter, the interplay of the static and the dynamic. In discussing these issues of spirituality, we must first, as Rupert Ross warns:

> ... be very careful when we consider the role of the spiritual plane. We are not dealing with some quaint custom, nor are we dealing with religion as many of us define that term in our post-industrial, western world. To many Native people, the spiritual plane is not simply a sphere of activity or belief which is separable from the pragmatics of everyday life; instead, it seems to be a context from within which most aspects [of] life are seen, defined and given significance.[xiv]

Keeping this in mind, it is then possible to begin to examine what I have come to understand as the way of reality.

Of all the topics in this book, I have spent the most time reflecting on the structure and process of life — a subject that genuinely intrigues me. Of all the subjects that I have discussed with my traditional Teachers, the structure and process of life has come up the most. I am still struggling with the lived-expression of *Mino-Bimaadiziwin*, but nevertheless will share the little I know here.

Anishinaabe *Mino-Bimaadiziwin* does not objectify the world creating artificial divisions of subject and object. It is difficult to understand this since we are constantly inundated with this subject/object dichotomy in the English language, but Anishinaabemowin is not noun-based but verb-based with the subject and object already encoded in the verb; meaning it is action- and relationship-oriented rather than subject/object oriented.[xv]

Anishinaabe *Mino-Bimaadiziwin* states that rather than a subject/object division reality is made up of dynamic and static aspects. One way to understand the dynamic and static aspects of reality is to imagine the experience of a new-born-child. Robert Pirsig, in *Lila: An Inquiry into Morals* (1991) explains that in the womb a baby is able to experience certain things such as pressure, sound and temperature among others. At birth, as they enter into the outside world, they acquire more complex experiences such as hunger, breath and light. As adults, we know these experiences as pressure, sound, temperature, hunger, light, and breathing and so on, but the baby does not. We call these experiences stimuli but the baby does not. From the perspective of the newborn child, that which draws his or her attention, such as hunger, is an undefined sensation and experience.

This generalized 'something', undefined, new and as yet unlabelled, is the dynamic aspect of reality. When the baby is a few months old he or she studies his or her hand with a sense of absolute wonder, mystery and excitement not knowing that it is a hand, or even that it is 'his or her' hand. There is no understanding of the perceived or the perceiver, no expression of possessed and possessor as the baby brings 'his or her' hand towards 'his or her' mouth. The distinction of self and 'things' out there is not a reality for the baby. As the baby becomes more and more attentive to the dynamic aspects of reality, he or she will begin to notice differences and likenesses and ultimately some kind of relationship between them. After a few months of playing with this wiggly 'thing' we adults call a hand, the baby will develop some kind of understanding of the 'out-thereness' of that hand.

Gradually the complex nature of that 'hand', through sensations and experiences and the baby's relationship with concepts like boundaries, distance and desire (although the baby does not categorize his or her experiences as concepts in the same sense adults do) will generate a general apprehension of something we call an object which can be reached for or observed out in space. This 'object', built up on static patterns of similarities and differences, and defined by 'its' relation to repeated experiences over time, that we call 'the hand' is not the primary experience for the baby. In fact, the primary experience for the baby is wonder, mystery and excitement. Once the baby has apprehended the complex pattern of experiences that are static in nature, called an object, and found this pattern to work in the same way repeatedly; i.e., it appears every time he or she brings the hand before his or her eyes, then the baby begins to develop a repertoire of knowledge about the world based on the repetition of certain events. As the baby's experiences continue, he or she begins to generalize these experiences thus developing the ability to jump through the chain of many small deductions based on repeated experience that produce the 'object' as though it were a single leap of reason.[xvi]

But at the same time, we must be cognizant that this apprehension of the outside world happens concurrently with the development of language for the baby. A child that is raised in an environment with a language that differentiates between subjects and objects will thus develop these categories in her/his lived-apprehension of the world. A child raised in an Anishinaabe environment will not develop these subject/object categories in the same way as western people perceive them since they do not exist in the same manner in Anishinaabe worldview. In Anishinaabemowin there is no need for an explicit reference to subjects or objects since their relationship is encoded in the verb. Nevertheless, subject/object relations are very important in spoken Anishinaabemowin and ultimately it is in the 'implicit naming' of these 'things' that there is a fundamental difference in language use and structure.[xvii]

Again, this is a very difficult idea to grasp for those of us raised with a worldview that distinguishes between subjects and objects. Many adults believe that subjects and objects are primary because they do not remember that time in their early life when they experienced the world as wonder, mystery and excitement. We believe that static patterns, unknowingly based on the many small forgotten dynamic experiential deductions made as a baby, *are* our reality of distinguishable subjects and objects. As we grow older and supposedly more knowledgeable of our environment, we move from primary dynamic experiences of wonder, mystery and excitement to basic static constructions of simple objects as well as distinctions like 'before' and 'after' and 'like' and unlike'. These simple static constructions grow into very complex constructions of cultures and beliefs with which we live. This is probably why children are usually quicker to perceive the dynamic aspects of the world than adults, why beginners are more open to new dynamic information than experts, and why Indigenous cultures are more in-tune with the dynamic aspects of Creation than so-called advanced technological societies.[xviii]

This is perhaps also part of the reason that the first European new-comers to this land referred to Aboriginal peoples as 'child-like' and why the tradition of paternalism became a central aim of Euro-American political and cultural assimilationist policies.

Absolutes and Non-singular Truths

Unlike subject/object metaphysics, Anishinaabe *Mino-Bimaadiziwin* does not insist on a single exclusive truth. If subjects and objects are held to be the ultimate reality, then we are permitted only one construction of things, these things corresponding only to the 'objective' world with all other constructions thus unreal. But if *Mino-Bimaadiziwin* is seen as the 'under-standing' of reality, it then becomes possible for more than one set of truths to exist. Marlene Brant Castellano (Mohawk) explains:

> Illustrating the personal nature of Aboriginal Knowledge, there is a story which has been repeated often enough to have a place in contemporary oral culture. At the hearings considering an injunction to stop the first James Bay Hydro-electric power development in Northern Québec, an Elder from one of the northern Cree communities potentially affected by the development was brought in to testify about Cree lifeways and the environment. He was asked to swear that he would tell the truth and he asked the translator for an explanation of the word. However truth was translated for him, as something which holds for all people, or something which is valid regardless of the rapporteur, the Elder responded: "I can't promise to tell you the truth; I can only tell you what I know."

> Aboriginal knowledge is rooted in personal experience and lays no claim to being universal. The degree to which you can trust what is being said is tied up with the integrity and perceptiveness of the speaker. If Joseph X reports that he saw signs of a moose in a

given direction, the information will be weighed in light of what is known of Joseph X, how often in the past his observations have proven accurate, what is known about this part of the territory, and the habits of moose. In any case, his observations would not necessarily be accepted uncritically, nor would they be contradicted or dismissed. They would be put in context.

The personal nature of knowledge means that disparate and even contradictory perceptions can be accepted as valid because they are unique to the person. In a council or talking circle of Elders you will not find arguments as to whose perception is more valid and therefore whose judgement should prevail. In other words, people do not contest with one another to establish who is correct, who has the "truth". Nevertheless, Aboriginal societies make a distinction between perceptions which are personal and wisdom which has social [and spiritual] validity and can serve as a basis for common action. Knowledge is validated through collective analysis and consensus-building.[xix]

One does not then seek the absolute truth since it is possible for more than one set of truths to exist. One seeks instead the highest good of life with the knowledge that if the past is any guide to the future this explanation must be taken conditionally: as useful until something better comes along. This 'something-better' for the Anishinaabeg is a further understanding of the traditional Teachings and how they are integrated into one's life. We each were sent to this Earth with Creator's Original Instructions encoded in our spirit. The ongoing unveiling of truth that happens throughout life is an unveiling of absolute truth

(Original Instructions). I believe in an absolute truth for a people, in this case the Anishinaabeg, as given by Creator. The word *Debwewin* (truth) at the core of *n'debewetawin* (the truth that is evident in the way of action) is a very powerful concept. I do not understand this truth as yet, but I know that it is at the core of my being. By 'absolute truth' I do not mean a truth that is the same for all individuals, but rather a sacred truth concerning the nature of Creation of which all beings are a part.

Learning is a life-long mission, where new knowledge is constantly added to knowledge learned yesterday. It is a path of self-actualization through a realization of *Gzhe-mnidoo*'s Original Instructions.

The Beauty Bridge

Because of the non-objectifying nature of Anishinaabe worldview, *Mino-Bimaadiziwin* reveals that one's life in static reality; that is, the everydayness of life or the mundane expression of perceived physical reality, finds its foundation on the dynamic unfolding of Creation. There is a bridge that links the static and the dynamic for the Anishinaabeg, and it is that of Beauty. Beauty is at the centre of the Anishinaabe perception of the world. It expresses the work of *Gzhe-mnidoo* in a way that allows a person to re-connect with the dynamic aspect of reality. When a person Fasts for a vision, dreams and/or sings a ceremonial song, to name a few activities, they are crossing the bridge of Beauty from the static to the dynamic. And when they cross back, as they must, they bring some of the dynamic into the static everydayness of this world.

It is said that a ceremonial song sung properly, for instance, gives wings to one's spirit.[xx] These wings allow one to cross the bridge of Beauty to the dynamic side. The song is described as beautiful, as an expression of *Gzhe-mnidoo*: the dynamic aspect. This aesthetic apprehension of reality allows one to discern the dynamic nature underlying the static appearance of the world.

The analogy of the bridge spanning between two areas is awkward; nevertheless, it is the closest that I can offer to describe what is, for all intents and purposes, non-describable. Creation is not a simple act of willing reality into being. The Anishinaabe Creation Story explains that there is a system of 'degrees' that would make up reality. Spiritual reality was created before the physical properties of the universe. The degrees, or 'steps' that were brought into being had to do, for example, with the fact that there is a difference between hot and cold, light and dark, and even female and male. It was decided that there could be no uniformity to reality; that it was essential that there be difference rather than sameness. In a non-differentiated universe there would be no reference to hot if there was no cold; light if there was no dark. In essence, we experience light/dark, hot/cold — without our experience they do not exist as such.[xxi]

We do, in fact, live in a differentiated universe. Anishinaabe metaphysics points out that this differentiation is essential to the way Creation works. However, the differentiation inherent in Anishinaabe philosophy is one of physical-spiritual or static-dynamic rather than subject/object. I am also aware that as I am writing this, I am writing from a static perspective.

There is a limitation in expressing these ideas since a spiritual apprehension of reality precedes and transcends static expressions of language and rationalization. When I say that the differentiation inherent in Anishinaabe philosophy is one of physical-spiritual or static-dynamic, I am stating this from a static perspective. It is essential that this static framework be acknowledged since there is no way to express the dynamic reality that is ultimately the 'way' of Creation. It is at this point that the counsels my Elders and traditional Teachers have given me about the limitation of this kind of work become most evident.

Thus, let me say simply that Anishinaabe *Mino-Bimaadiziwin* is a process, a way of a good life. It is understood that this way of life goes beyond a simple intellectual exercise of examination, discussion and description. *Mino-Bimaadiziwin* also includes the lived-process of Primary Experiential Knowledge actualized through living; i.e., 'the way' of the Way of a Good Life.

Notes

[1] Bourgeois, "An Ojibwe Conceptual Glossary", 12.

[2] *Mino-Bimaadiziwin* is a compound word made up of *Mino* (good, nice, well), *bimaadizi* (live, be alive) and the ending *win* (the way of being). *Bimaadizid* is also the proper term for 'a human being". There is also a reference in *Bimaadiziwin* to following or going along as on a path.

[3] Benton-Banai, *The Mishomis Book, Voice of the Ojibway*, 29.

[4] See Edward Benton-Banai, *The Mishomis Book, Voice of the Ojibway*, for an account of the birth of the Second People.

[5] Ibid., 60.

[6] Dumont, "Journey To Daylight-Land Through Ojibwa Eyes", 75.

[7] Couture, "The Role of Native Elders: Emergent Issues", (passim)

[8] See Figure 3

[9] See Figure 4

[10] There is a tradition of treatment of disease but this tradition is beyond the scope of this book.

[11] Rémi Savard, *Destin à'Amerique. Les Autochtones et nous* (Montréal: Édition de l'Hexagone, 1979) ,15. (lib. trans. by author)

[12] Traditional Teacher, conversation with author, 1996.

[13] Dumont, "Journey To Daylight-Land Through Ojibwa Eyes", 78.

[14] Rupert Ross, *Dancing with a Ghost, Exploring Indian Reality* (Ontario, Octopus, 1992), 54-55.

[15] Brian McInnis, conversation with author, 1998.

[16] Robert Pirsig, *Lila, An Inquiry Into Morals* (New York: Bantam Books, 1992), 137. (passim)

[17] Brian McInnis, conversation with author, 1998.

[18] Pirsig, *Lila, An Inquiry Into Morals*, 137-138.(passim)

[19] Marlene Brant Castellano, "Updating Aboriginal Traditions of Knowledge" in *Indigenous Knowledge: Multiple Readings of Our World* (Toronto: University of Toronto Press, forthcoming, 1998), TMs [photocopy], 6-7.

[20] Traditional Teacher, conversation with author, 1997.

[21] Traditional Teacher, conversation with author, 1997.

Chapter 6

Eyaa'oyaanh

I t is my hope that the preceding chapters have prepared you for this final chapter. My examination of *Kendaaswin* and the various sources of knowledge coupled with discussions about cultural stories, traditional Teachings, Creation as unity, and the actualization of life all led directly to the previous section on the dynamic-static view of reality. This view of reality aids us in understanding the underlying purpose of life; i.e., good life. What follows is my attempt to describe what a good life is for an individual.

Eyaa'oyaanh literally means "the way that everything is in me, or, every way I am of my being, of the quality of my existence"[ii.] *Mino-Bimaadiziwin* is the process of a person trying to be or exist in this good way.

The Path of Life

The Path of Life that is *Mino-Bimaadiziwin* can best be described as the ideal path set out for me by *Gzhe-mnidoo*. As a free individual I have the choice to follow this ideal path. The Path of Life is the potential of my life, lived in a good way. For me, life is a process within a process: a lived-existence within Creation. It is taught that I am an integral aspect of Creation, and that my place therein is set out in a potential way by *Gzhe-mnidoo*. The potentiality of my life, moreover my good life, can only be set into motion, or more to the point, actualized, through a process of *Nwenamdanwin* (choice-making) and *N'dendowin* (responsibility-taking). It is shown that making choices in life is the only way to actualize the potentiality of Creation. As such, I am Creation manifest and must be consciously aware of my place and purpose within that creative process. Since this Path is ideal, I have to choose to actualize it, to make it real.

It is taught that there are Seven Stages of life; namely, birth-good life (birth to 6), Fast life (7-13), wondering-wandering (14-20), truth (21-27), planning-planting (28-34), doing (35-41), and traditional Teacher, Elder-hood and death (42 to the end of life).[iii] The ages attributed to these stages are not absolute but rather possible indicators of various stages. The Seven Stages are a continuum on the Path of Life.

Birth-good life is so called since the infant has all his/her needs taken care of by the family and community. Fast life refers to the adolescent years when a person has the tendency to act without reflected thought. There are many factors at play during this period including new sexual urges, the preparation of one's place in society, new skills, knowledge, and duties. The wondering and wandering years are the years of early adulthood. These years find a young person developing a more refined faculty of observation and inquiry concerning the world at large. It is in these years that a person uncovers one's role and purpose in life. The years of truth find a person as a full adult, taking on the duties and responsibilities of this age. People discover that they 'fit' into their world and begin to fulfil their potential as a good person.

The years of planning and planting are the years of raising a family and of adding to the community in a constructive way. The years of doing are those years where one's family has grown up so that one is able to spend more time on personal concerns. This is a period of renewed balance and of further exploration of the spiritual and intellectual aspects of life. Finally, the years of being a traditional Teacher, and then gradually over time an Elder, are taken up with sharing one's life experience, of teaching and helping others find their ideal path in life. The Elder is able to perceive the unity of the physical-spiritual world in a way only gained with life experience. As a person reaches greater age they move towards the spiritual realm, gradually leaving behind the physicality of the world. At the end of one's life, one's death reveals the added dimension of the spirit world; a world where pure spirit exists. It is in this realm that the unity of the physical-spiritual is fully revealed.

These stages of life are set out in an ordered fashion so that the development of a person is structured within the culture. In these contemporary times, there are many Anishinaabeg that discover their Path of Life at an older age, such as I did. These prescribed stages are still applied, and a person new to this traditional way is initially considered a newborn. They are helped along by the Elders and Teachers, as a child would be. Since they are adults, their progression along the path is, at times, faster; whereby the Teachings and reflections thereon are learned at a faster pace. Yet, one's sense of perception; i.e., Anishinaabe perception, is compromised and not fully developed in those adults who may begin on their traditional path later in life.

This compromise is due to the contemporary experience of the Anishinaabe person living in a foreign and dominant non-Native society that makes the learning and process of choice-making very difficult. It is understood that many Anishinaabeg come from a social and political environment that may limit the information necessary to make a reflected choice. Consequently, the Elders and traditional Teachers recognize this, and special provisions are taken with regard to Teachings and their presentation. This is not to say that the Teachings are rushed, only that they are given in such a way that a person is able to progress smoothly along the path. The Anishinaabeg pre-occupy themselves with the process of helping people heal their lives. All Teachings still happen in an ordered fashion, and the life experience of the new person is necessarily taken into consideration.

The Anishinaabe culture is witness to many people rediscovering their traditions and ceremonies, and it is taught that the people are part of a Spiritual Renaissance that was spoken of long ago. All are responsible for the next seven generations of Anishinaabeg, and, as such, they learn these traditional ways in order to raise their own children in an appropriate manner so that these children may, in turn, do so with their own children.

As one moves through the stages of life that make up one's life-path one finds that there are side paths which branch off. These side paths are also potential. It is on these life-tangents that one can find such distractions as greed, power, lust, resentment, anger, pity, self-centredness, low self-esteem, jealousy, substance abuse, etc. These side paths are different for each individual. At times, these side paths are beneficial to a person's overall knowledge of life, but only if one is able to return to the path that leads one forward in life and there integrate these lessons in one's life. It is said that some people may get lost on these side paths and literally run out of time, unable to find their way back. The path that leads one forward in life as well as the side paths (distractions) are all part of the ideal path that we must each navigate.

Determination and Freedom

When discussing the Path of Life and the Seven Stages it is easy to assume that my life is somehow determined; that, ultimately, I have no real choice in my life pursuit. At first glance it can be seen how this conclusion could be reached; nevertheless, the concept of *Waanizhijigeyaanh* (free will) plays a central role in the Anishinaabe concept of identity. Personal identity, for the Anishinaabeg, is defined as the underlying potentiality of a person. Creator sends my spirit before conception. My spirit has everything that I need to live a good life. As I live my life, I discover what my spirit holds by choosing to examine and follow this good way of life. Ultimately, my reality is within and not outside. It is said that a person that traditionally expressed a given talent or ability for the task at hand; e.g., hunting, Lodge building, ceremonies, etc., would be the natural leader for that task. It is recognized that each person has a 'speciality' that they are best at, and it is their responsibility to perform that task to the best of their ability. In so doing, the ability to do good is recognized, but implicitly, the potential of being good is also actualized. For contemporary Anishinaabeg that base their lives on traditional Teachings, this is still true.

A World of Relations

One of the things that I have been taught by my traditional Teachers is that I am at the centre of a community of relations that moves from my immediate family to the whole of the population of the world, this population including humans and non-humans alike.[iv] This is my reality as a person. It is based on the traditional Anishinaabe teaching of the interelatedness of all beings with *Eshkakimikwe*.

An underlying truth for the Anishinaabeg is the inherent relationship, and belief in a relationship, with our Earth Mother. The Anishinaabeg are spiritually bound in this relationship, and this relationship defines each being as a child of Mother. This is not some kind of mystical awareness that comes only from a Ceremony or a ritual; it comes from the very essence of Anishinaabe worldview and thought. Anishinaabe philosophy also stresses the importance of *Kendaaswin*. *Kendaaswin*, or the way of learning, is the epistemic source of this truth.

The Anishinaabe person is a practitioner of *Mino-Bimaadiziwin*; in other words she or he is a dynamic empiricist. Dynamic empiricism is the process by which I come to understand the world through an expanded perception that encompasses the physical-spiritual reality of Creation. But this world is seen as more than the simple subject/object structure that is often spoken of in Western philosophies. It is an apprehension of the dynamic nature of Creation. The Anishinaabeg do not look at the world as being made up of subjects and objects but rather understand that goodness, value and beauty are primary.

As the centre of a community of relations, my understanding of the world grows from my Primary Experiential Knowledge. This is not a relativistic statement but the statement of a person who is learning and practicing the traditional ways of his people. All my knowledge is verified through a system of Elders and traditional Teachers whose life knowledge allows them to discern the dynamic nature of Creation. The value of Primary Experiential Knowledge, be it from cultural stories, traditional and ceremonial instructions, observation of the world, or from dreams, visions and intuition, is verifiable since there is no subject/object bifurcation inherent in Anishinaabe worldview. Metaphysically, in the West, the value of Primary Experiential Knowledge, particularly knowledge received from a spiritual source, has been generally discounted due to the belief that the universe is composed of subjects and objects. If something cannot be classified as one or the other then it does not exist and is relegated to relativism, conjecture, belief and faith. It has also been discounted due to the belief that it is not quantifiable and reproducible in a 'controlled' environment. This is a metaphysical assumption. Anishinaabe metaphysics does not make this subject/object assumption. Robert Pirsig explains that:

> This problem of trying to describe [this] value [the dynamic] in terms of substance [the static] has been the problem of a small container trying to contain a larger one. Value is not a subspecies of substance. Substance is a subspecies of value. When you reverse the containment process and define substance in terms of value the mystery disappears ...[v]

We are taught that each Spirit enters the physical world complete. The Spirit that I express carries with it my name, my Clan, my gifts and my purpose in life. When I say *Mino-Bimaadiziwin*, I am speaking of the Way of a Good Life, not as an individual subject separate from other objects or subjects in the world, but as a unified aspect of Creation.

Existence and Being Good

Generally, there is a fairly evident division between Western and Anishinaabe conceptions of existence. Joseph Couture (Cree/Métis) explains that:

> In the West, classical existentialism stresses the utter validity of subjectivity, i.e., of the feeling, reflective subject who has the freedom to make choices, and to determine thus his/her life. Therefore, what one does is of keystone importance. The doing that characterizes the Native Way is a doing that concerns itself with being and becoming a unique person, one fully responsible for one's own life and actions within

family and community. Finding one's path and following it is a characteristic Native enterprise which leads to or makes for the attainment of inner and outer balance. This is a marked contrast with general Western doing which tends and strains towards having, objectifying, manipulating, 'thingifying' every one and every thing it touches.[vi]

Couture (Cree/Métis) points out that the 'doing' of life for the Anishinaabe person is one of being and becoming good. It is a way of life that is both spiritual and ethical. Choice exists for both the Western and Anishinaabe person, but it seems to me that the Anishinaabe person has the added dimension of following an ideal path rather than creating the path itself. Choice is a tool of actualization rather than of invention. Again, the main concern is of being good rather than simply doing good. This fact is found in another translation of the name of the people, "Anishinaabe": the Good Being.[vii]

Anishinaabe philosophy also stresses the interconnectivity of Creation rather than the connectivity of a physical and spiritual world. The Western tradition, from the time of the Greek philosopher Plato (428-348 B.C.E.), has attempted to divide reality into a rigid duality. Plato posited a two-world metaphysics of the intelligible and the sensible with a very clear division between the two. The French philosopher René Descartes (1596-1650) later refined this idea to a separation of mind or soul and body. The Anishinaabeg do not separate the mind and body. There is an understanding of the person as a whole lived being. There is mention of the four aspects of the lived person; namely, mind, body, spirit and emotion, but they are not seen as independent, separate divisions.[viii]

At first glance it would seem there is also a synthesis of the physical and the spiritual in Anishinaabe philosophy. But as we have seen in the previous section on the dynamic-static, the Anishinaabeg understand reality as transcendent where the physical and the spiritual are merely aspects of the whole rather than parts that make up the whole.

In the same manner as above, the Creator-Creation equation transcends a simple synthesis since it stresses the great Circle of Life. In the Creation Story, it is taught that before creating the universe, *Gzhe-mnidoo* first sent out thoughts to see if there was anything or anyone else. After a great deal of time and with no contact, *Gzhe-mnidoo* retrieved those thoughts, and today there are stars where they ended their journey.[ix] Like *Gzhe-mnidoo*'s journey in thought through the universe, the Great Circle of Life entails a journey of discovery of my physical-spiritual world and my place therein.

Within the cycle of birth and death it is evident that everything that exists has a beginning and an end. For the Anishinaabeg, the divinity of life is paramount. Nevertheless, the Anishinaabeg are not simply animistic. It is not a simple matter of saying that all is alive; that there is no inanimate. Rather, it must be understood that all is animate potentially, and that this life can be actualized in various fashions, but always by way of choice-making. As such, I find myself part of a vast community called Creation, immediately connected to all its aspects. For non-human beings, the path of life unveils itself in a simple direct manner, but I must work harder at following the path. Humans are beings that have the tendency to wander about, unlike non-humans that are more directed due to their state of existence. Humans are considered the weakest being in the world. Each human needs a great deal of help in finding the potential of his/her life path, and even more help in learning to actualize it. We are not necessarily in tune with our intuitive abilities and, as such, struggle somewhat.

In Creation, one is never alone. The divine is everywhere. Everything received is a gift since at each level I am in a personal relationship with Creation. Everything — all action, all thought, all emotions — have a personal texture and import. Nevertheless, I am not anonymous in an impossibly crowded world such as we know today. I am unique: the only example of myself. My sense of uniqueness, my unique ability to choose and act, underlies my very existence. My moral agency gives me a sense of dignity and I express this in taking complete responsibility for my choices. The Creator sets out an ideal Path of Life for each being. It is my path in-so-far that I may or may not choose to actualize it as I live.

In the Anishinaabe life-way, I must be aware of all my relations, human and non-human, and as such there is a rich sense of community. I am never alone. Moreover, individual accountability and understanding are intimately interrelated since only I can understand: nobody else can make me find the truth within.

Ultimately, this all comes down to what James Dumont calls a special way of seeing the world whereby there must be a comprehensive, total viewing of the world.[x] This special way of seeing the world involves the ability to 'see' the potential therein. The Anishinaabeg have always understood that the place of humans in this world is only that of one type of being among many others.

The creative power of existence always nurtures the life that is created. Ultimately, existence is totally dependent on Creation. This dependence on the divine power of Creation is fundamental and as such there is a general sense that nothing that exists can be taken for granted. All is divine by the very nature of Creation. There is also the knowledge that the divine power of Creation can be trusted, and that all things are where they belong. This is evident in the knowledge that all things happen in their own way, for their own reasons. As such, Creation is meaningful and ordered.

The divinity and order of Creation makes every moment precious and there is a sense of gratitude and humility (very important aspects of *Mino-Bimaadiziwin*) for this reality. Since all existence is divine, all existence has a direct link to Creator and

Creation. The interconnectivity of all life, potential and actual, makes the world a safe and meaningful place where I am able to explore and ultimately fully actualize my identity.

Oshkaabewis

Anishinaabe philosophy explains that there is an ideal person: *Oshkaabewis* or 'the new one'. This term is used for the ceremonial male helpers (the female helpers are called *Gichitwaakwe*) as a way of teaching the purpose of life, although conceptually *Oshkaabewis* is neither male nor female. The ideal person, *Oshkaabewis*, gives men and women an example of how one can be a good person.

To be a good person I must respect and love the Elders, women and children as the centre of the cultural circle; and, in effect, loving and respecting all living beings. To be respectful I must be honest in my purpose. Honesty comes from truth and the courage to be truthful. The greatest pride of the Anishinaabeg is their unwavering truthfulness. Honesty, courage and truth are evident only through trust; trust in myself as a good person, trust in others and in Creation. Ultimately all the aspects of a good life are based on moderation and humility. A good life is defined by moderation; i.e., moderation of desire and purpose as well as behaviour. This sense of moderation and humility has many times been perceived as shyness or timidity by non-Natives; but, in fact, is the expression of a respectful person.[xi]

Mino-Bimaadiziwin, 'the way of the Path of Life', and *Oshkaabewis*, 'the new one' are two of the major tenets of Anishinaabe philosophy. These are given to differentiate between 'doing good' and 'being good'. The purpose of a good life is not to simply do good, since this is only the outward expression of action. I must go to the centre of my being, like the centre of the Seven Directions Medicine Wheel, and there find goodness.[xii] Being good is the actualization of the potentiality of the Path of Life, of *Gzhe-mnidoo*'s Original Instructions. Being good means that I have made reflected choices and that I have taken full responsibility for those choices.[xiii]

The Medicine Wheel

The Medicine Wheel is the template that allows a systematic discovery of the varying aspects of *Mino-Bimaadiziwin*. The Medicine Wheel is a tool, and a dynamic tool at that. There is no definitive Medicine Wheel that is used by all Aboriginal people. In fact, there is no definitive wheel used by all Anishinaabeg as a whole. As a static representation, it moves in real time and space. As such, there is no absolute position of any division. The wheel conceptually divides what is interconnected in Creation. It allows a person the ability to grasp the utter complexity of Creation in small, manageable pieces so that they can begin to reflect on various aspects, and then move to the next. Traditionally, the Medicine Wheel is divided into seven directions; namely, the four cardinal directions, the direction above, below and the centre.[xiv] It is said that a person goes to each of the six outward directions to find a new Teaching, either actually or symbolically. In early age these Teachings come to the child, but as that person grows older they venture out themselves. This is evident in the third stage of life where the young person wonders and wanders, searching out new knowledge and answers.

Gradually, a person always returns to the *nisaway'ayiing* (centre), the seventh direction, to reflect on the Teachings and integrate those lessons into his or her life. This is where I find myself. This is the direction that I return to after travelling to the outward directions. This is the place of spiritual balance.

Gzhe-mnidoo

In Anishinaabe philosophy, the divine is always central. The thing that differentiates this philosophical tradition from those of the West is the fact that *Gzhe-mnidoo* is both immanent as well as transcendent. By immanent, I mean that *Gzhe-mnidoo* is in the world or universe. By transcendent, I mean that *Gzhe-mnidoo* also lies outside of Creation as the unlimited divine power that defines 'Being'. Like the Elder who is both librarian and library of traditional knowledge, *Gzhe-mnidoo* is both the actor and the action of Creation. *Gzhe-mnidoo* is the all of Creation and the one. This seeming duality of immanence and transcendence can be further understood as unity in movement. Once Creation is no longer seen as some kind of differentiated substantiality but as unity, a state of physical-spiritual balance is found.

In our discussion of the Anishinaabeg's orientation concerning *Mino-Bimaadiziwin* we have come to understand its place in the lived experience of a person's life. We have reviewed the underlying philosophical structures that delineate the process of life, consequently uncovering the 'process of the process', or the horizon or ground upon which life is able to find its footing. Each person is potentially the *Oshkaabewis* understanding the meaning of *Mino-Bimaadiziwin*. My task in life is to express the good being that lies within. Consequently, I can unleash the power of truth, uncovering the possibility of a balanced life and of the realization that life is a process, within the process of Creation. This good is found in the simple act of choice-making; i.e., doing good. However, it is the ability of wisdom, love, respect, courage, honesty, humility, moderation, and truth that allows me to take complete responsibility for those choices; i.e., being good. As I have come to realize, the Path of Life is set out as pure potentiality by *Gzhe-mnidoo*, whereby it is my responsibility to make reasoned choices for its actualization and take responsibility for those choices. As such, I am always free to choose.

Consequently, the Anishinaabeg do not see *Mino-Bimaadiziwin* as something that lies within the realm of simple process, but rather, that *Mino-Bimaadiziwin* is the way as well as the result, the means and the end, of being a good person.

Notes

---

[1] Couture, "The Role of Native Elders: Emergent Issues", 205.

[2] Brian McInnis, conversation with author, 1998.

[3] Edna Manitowabi, conversation with author, 1997.

[4] See Figure 3

[5] Pirsig, *Lila, An Inquiry Into Morals*, 116.

[6] Couture, "The Role of Native Elders: Emergent Issues", 207.

[7] Brian McInnis, conversation with author, 1998.

[8] See Figure 4

[9] See Edward Benton-Banai, *The Mishomis Book, Voice of the Ojibway*. The Creation story also tells us that Creator, in the creation of Earth, had to try more than once before getting the formula right for life. Any philosophy that posits a non-omniscient and non-omnipotent Creator must, by its very nature, be radically different than anything found in Western traditions. I am not saying that *Gzhe-mnidoo* is incompetent but rather that the nature of learning is universal – even for the creator of this learning.

[10] Dumont, "Journey To Daylight-Land Through Ojibwa Eyes", 78. (passim)

[11] Elder, conversation with author, 1996.

[12] See Figure 2

[13] Elder, conversation with author, 1996.

[14] See Figure 2

Conclusion

I t is now the early part of the summer of 1998. After spending so much time writing, I can feel in my heart that I have said everything I know about Anishinaabe philosophy. Yet, it remains my intention to continue learning the philosophy of the Anishinaabeg and I am firm in my belief that it must be recognized as one of the great philosophies of the world. However, the comprehensive document that I had envisioned early on as I first sat down to write these words does not yet exist. This is, perhaps, only a first step towards that goal.

In the Introduction I wrote that Anishinaabe conceptions of reality still remain true to the Original Instructions of *Gzhe-mnidoo* and the traditions that have been passed down through countless generations. Now that I have finished my work I realize how true this statement actually is. New generations of Anishinaabeg are gradually beginning to discuss their traditions in a new way, in the written form and in the English language; but, the core of those Teachings is unchangeable, eternal and sacred. I may have thought that I was re-inventing the wheel when I decided to write about something that had never been written before, but I now realize that I have only spoken about concepts and ideas as countless others have done before me. The fact that I have discussed some of these ideas makes no difference to the traditions of my ancestors. I have a keen awareness, as I re-read what I have written, that I am connected to a line of knowledge that is older than time itself. I am fortunate that I have been able to learn some of this Way of a Good Life.

The long-standing conversation concerning the writing of Anishinaabe philosophy goes on. I asked myself many times if I was doing the right thing by writing this book. I was made aware, early in my work, of the serious limitations to revealing 'sacred' knowledge and even the personal learning I have done in my life. As a rule, the Teachings that remain part of the oral ceremonial traditions upon which I base this work were not made available here, since I was taught that people cannot possibly 'feel' the power of these Teachings from these pages written in English. My Teachers have impressed on me that it is essential that these Teachings be experienced through the traditional Ceremonies in the original language of the Anishinaabeg. Again, the context and protocol of the place and time that the Teachings are given, who gives the Teaching, as well as the ceremonial presence of the Spirit of these Teachings ensures that they never become static in presentation and meaning.

The fact that Anishinaabe philosophy is based on a system of interconnection forced me to disconnect various concepts and ideas from the whole so that I could examine them. I struggled long and hard with the structural organization of this work. This was the greatest difficulty I faced in writing this book. I felt that if I did not discuss the concepts in a certain way, in a certain order, it would be akin to pulling a piece of yarn in a sweater and having the whole thing come unravelled in my hands.

I think that the categorizations and structures that I have developed in this work fulfil many of the necessary needs of academia. Now that I look back on what I have written, I realize that it is far more academic than I had originally thought it would be. I know, from conversations with Elders and traditional Teachers, that the organization of this book is far from being traditional in nature. In academic thinking, the categorizations made here may make sense but for those most knowledgeable of Anishinaabe traditions, this work has a curious structure since it divides and separates ideas and concepts that are fundamentally interconnected. After reading the first draft of this book a friend said, "I wonder what would have been the response of my great-grandfather to such categorization."[i]

As I noted earlier, the sensing of my 'self' and my cultural intuition are what led me to develop a different method of investigation. I have used a method of learning and sharing based on recognized Anishinaabe protocols. The use of "Applied Anishinaabe Theory" as the foundation of my "Primary Experiential Knowledge" method has allowed me to investigate this process-oriented philosophy; discussing various facets of Anishinaabe culture, history, metaphysics, ontology, epistemology, axiology, aesthetics and identity that I felt were key to the understanding I have of *Mino-Bimaadiziwin*. Since Anishinaabe philosophy is based on a fundamental way of knowing, a fundamental epistemology, any non-qualitative method would have rendered this study invalid by the very nature of what I was studying. As I stated previously, in the case of my research dealing with the Way of a Good Life, knowledge and identity, my method not only develops the necessary structures for this investigation, but also provides a degree of self-revelation about me as an individual.

Now that my research, process of reflection and writing is over, I realize how great the degree of self-revelation has been. The knowledge that I wrote of in this book continues to have a profound impact on me. It is a knowledge that is not only about me — but is me. It is my whole identity, all my thoughts, dreams, wishes and goals. In essence, it is what motivates and defines my life. The unbroken line of knowledge that I referred to is all of this — an unbroken line of feelings which I am 'plugged into'. When I first felt this reconnection on hearing the drum at the Sweat Lodge Ceremony, all I could do was cry. That is the feeling in the knowledge that I am reconnected with.

It is true that any study of any philosophy will provide a significant degree of self-exploration and revelation, but the nature of the knowledge that I have attempted to examine here is different. This knowledge represents the means of achieving the deepest form of subjective understanding there is, since the method of Primary Experiential Knowledge that I use allows me to discover objective truths through a necessarily inter-subjective method of inquiry and analysis explicitly characteristic of Anishinaabe protocols. Again, since it is not possible for me to separate myself from the world, particularly the knowledge of that world, I have used a qualitative methodological inquiry based on a blending of participant observation and participant participation that incorporates and recognizes my thoughts, experiences, reflections, emotions, and spirituality in my personal life.

I return to my traditional Teachers, once-in-a-while like Elder Louis Crier suggested, showing them the moose that I have found. As it turns out, there is a vast herd of moose out there and I know there is not enough time in my life to find them all. I must, I think, decide which moose to pursue. Many of us may pursue the same one and then be able to share that knowledge with others. And others may help by saying, "If you go that way you won't find a moose. But, if you go that way, you will."[ii] And still others may choose to pursue very rare moose, perhaps only seen once or twice in a generation. Ultimately, there are far too many moose for me to follow, let alone the enormous amount of time and energy it takes to pursue just one. If I am not careful in my pursuit, I may forever walk in circles. Interestingly, that is what the Anishinaabe word for the hunt — *giiwosewin* — actually means. Quite simply, I need to pick my moose and follow him or her very closely and learn that path of knowledge. I am very fortunate that each moose I do meet takes the time to teach me everything he or she knows. These never-ending gifts allow me to better understand *Mino-Bimaadiziwin.*

Notes

_____

[1] Brian McInnis, conversation with author, 1998.
[2] Couture, "Native Studies and the Academy", 3.

Glossary

Sounds and Orthography[i]

The system of spelling used in this glossary follows the style devised by Charles Fiero. In the description of Anishinaabe sounds, some English and French words are given to approximate Anishinaabe pronunciation. Double vowels represent long spoken sounds and apostrophes represent short pauses in the pronunciation of the word.

Anishinaabe alphabetical order: a, aa, b, c, d, e, g, h, ', i, ii, j, k, m, n, o, oo, p, s, t, w, y, z

Short Vowels: a — about; i — pin; o - obey

Long Vowels: aa — father; e — café; ii — seen; oo — boat

Consonants and their sound: b — big; ch — stitch; d — between do and stop; g — between geese and ski; h — hi; j — jump;

k — pick; m — man; n — name; p — rip; s — miss; sh — bush; t — pit; w — way; y — yellow; z — zebra; zh ⁃ measure

Nasal Vowels: aanh — as in the French maman; enh — as in the French père; iinh — as in the French matin; oonh — as in the French bonbon

Anishinaabe Kendaaswin: Traditional Anishinaabe knowledge. Knowledge that is passed down from generation to generation in a ceremonial environment.

Anishinaabe: *pl* Anishinaabeg. The good being (male) created from nothing and lowered down to Earth. Name of all people who are descendants of the people who speak various dialects of Anishinaabemowin.

Anishinaabemowin: The Anishinaabe language.

Asemaa: Tobacco.

Asin: *pl* asiniig, Rock, stone.

Aadizookaan: Traditional cultural story.

Aazhikenimonenaadizid Bemaadizid: The study of the behaviour of life.

Biimadizid: A human being.

Bzindamowin: Acquired knowledge. Learning from listening. Knowledge that is shared through cultural stories.

Chinshinabe: pl Chinshinabeg. Those beings that comprehend the Ancient Great Mystery of the 'good' way of life, of the essence of existence. The Ancient Ones.

Debwewin: Truth.

Dewe'gan: *pl* dewe'ganag, Drum.

Enadizewin: Natural law. The natural way of behaviour. The way of life that is on land. Includes all aspects of living based on Creator's Original Instructions.

Eshkakimikwe: Mother Earth.

Eyaa'oyaanh: Identity. The way everything is in me or every way I am of my being. Who I am.

Gchi Makade Makwa: A Large black bear.

Gichitwaakwe: A female ceremonial helper.

Gidisi'ewin: Intuition. The navel way. Mother connection in you.

Gnawaaminjigewin: Knowledge from observation. To look, to see, to witness. Following the knowledge from somebody. Seeing what is being done.

Gzhe-mnidoo: The Creator.

Kendaaswin: Knowledge. Learning as in the way of counting.

Kenjigadewin: Reality. Reality of a fact. A known truth.

Kiimiingona manda Kendaaswin: The Original Instructions given to the Anishinaabeg by Gzhe-mnidoo.

Makadeke: The act of Fasting.

Makadekewigaan: A Fasting Lodge.

Makadekewin: Fasting or vision quest. The way of the vision quest.

Manidoo waabiwin: Revealed knowledge. Seeing in a spirit way.

Manidoo: *pl* manidoog. A spirit.

Manidooke: Conduct a Ceremony.

Manidookewin: A Ceremony.

Minidoo-minjimendamowin: Spirit memory/blood memory. Stitched into your spirit. The knowledge that enters this world when one's spirit fuses with the physical body. Spirit identity.

Minjimendamowin: Memory. Hold in and stitch together.

Mino-Bimaadiziwin: The Way of a Good Life. In order to have a good life one must have a goal. This goal is to be free from illness, to live to the fullest. Bimaadiziwin is based on a concept of health and good living. One must work on prevention and not only healing. It is a Holy Life. One must eat well, act well, and live physically, mentally, emotionally and spiritually well. Emotional well-being is a key to Bimaadiziwin.

Mishkiki: Medicine that comes from the roots of Earth.

Mishkikiwin: The way of medicine. The way of medicine includes prayer, song, dancing, Ceremony, plants, Fasting, dreams and the Sweat Lodge.

Mishoomis: *pl* mishoomisag. Grandfather.

N'debewetawin: Belief. The truth that is evident in the way of the action. One cannot know the truth unless one has seen or experienced it in a direct way (physically or spiritually).

N'debewewin: Faith. The heart that everything relates too. Truthfulness.

N'dendowin: Responsibility. My responsibility of a choice I made.

Naanaagede'enmowin: A spiritual vision. Like a meditation, reason through meditation. Sorting your thoughts out.

Naapewewin/naademowin: Vivid dream — lucid.

Nebwakawin: Wisdom. From the root 'nebwa' — in the kindness of putting yourself backwards but at the same time of bringing forward the wisdom one carries. Thinking back, bringing forward and stitching all together; i.e., life knowledge (Elders).

Nendaamowin: Forget. Unstitched.

Nenemowin: Thought. The will or power of a thought.

Nisaway'ayiing: At the centre.

Noodin: Be windy. Also the term used to describe the mind.

Nookomis: *pl* nookomisag. Grandmother.

Nwenamdan: Choice. Browsing in one's thoughts. I am seeking to make a decision of what pleases me.

Nwenamdanwin: Making a choice.

O'de: Heart.

Odewegewin: The way of the drum.

Oshkaabewis: The New One. A male ceremonial helper.

Waanizhijigeyaanh: Free-will. The way I am going to do things [the action].

Wanenenema: Will. Has to do with the ability to think independently.

Wiigiwaamaatig: Lodge pole.

Zaagedewin: Love/caring. All of something emanating out of you [from the root 'to bloom']. Not the same sense as the English 'make love' (sexual) but rather of caring. It is something based on mutual respect. You can feel it but you cannot touch it. It is all of you filling the heart of another (m'nadenemowin: feeding that heart with the thought of something). Out of Zaagedewin a human being is able to heal him/her self.

Zhiishiigwan: *pl* zhiishiigwanag, Shaker, rattle.

Notes

---

[1] See John D. Nichols and Earl Nyholm. *A Concise Dictionary of Minnesota Ojibwe* (Minnesota: University of Minnesota Press, 1995), xxiv-xxviii.

Illustrations

Figure 1. Anishinaabe Language Map

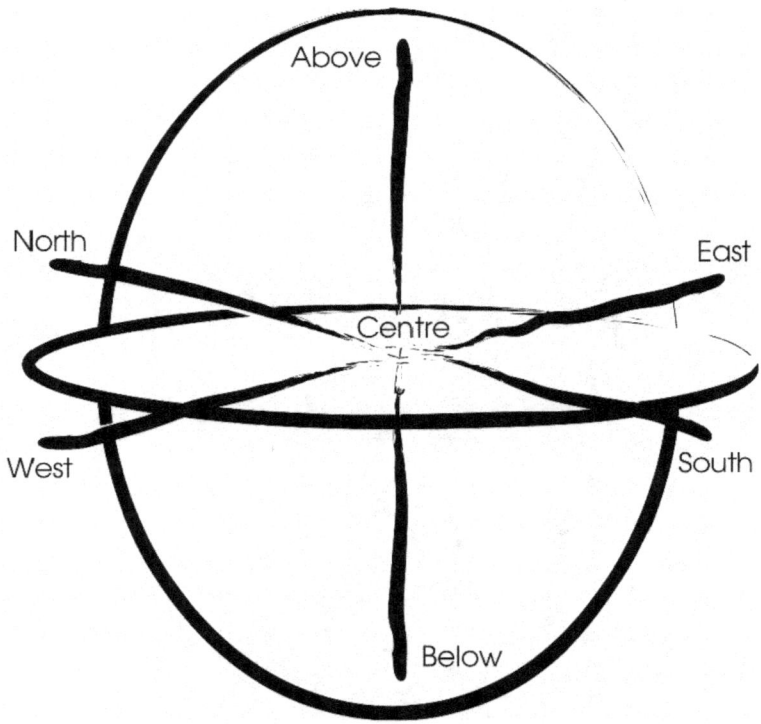

Figure 2 A Medicine Wheel (7 Directions)[i]

This is a graphic representation of the seven cardinal directions. Each direction has corresponding Teachings about medicines, animals, spirits, powers, physical elements, gifts, knowledge, time and life stages, to name but a few. These Teachings remain within the realm of Oral knowledge.

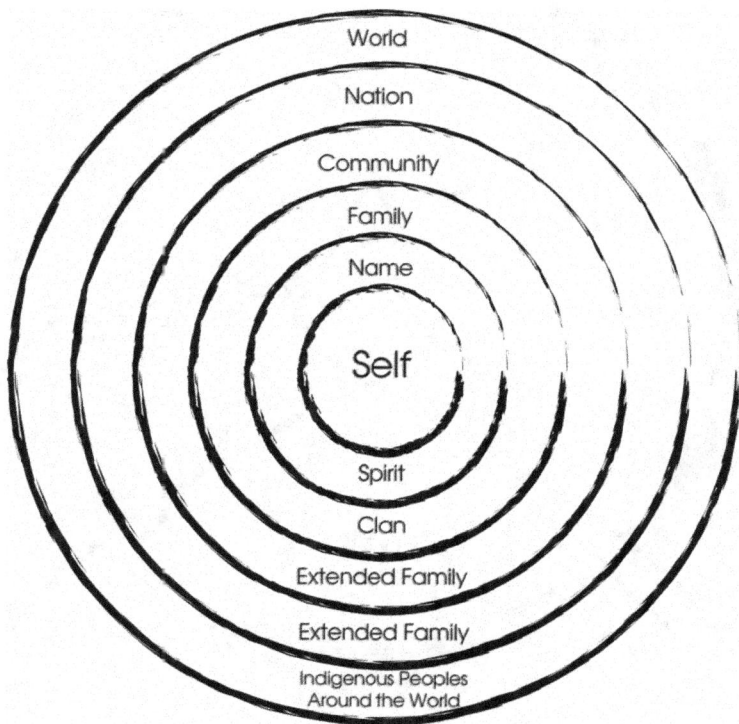

Figure 3. A World of Relations[ii]

The relationships that are represented here include all worldly and spiritual relations (spirit, mineral, plant, animal, insect, and human life). Each expanded circle outward from the self corresponds to Teachings and explanations that remain within the realm of Oral knowledge.

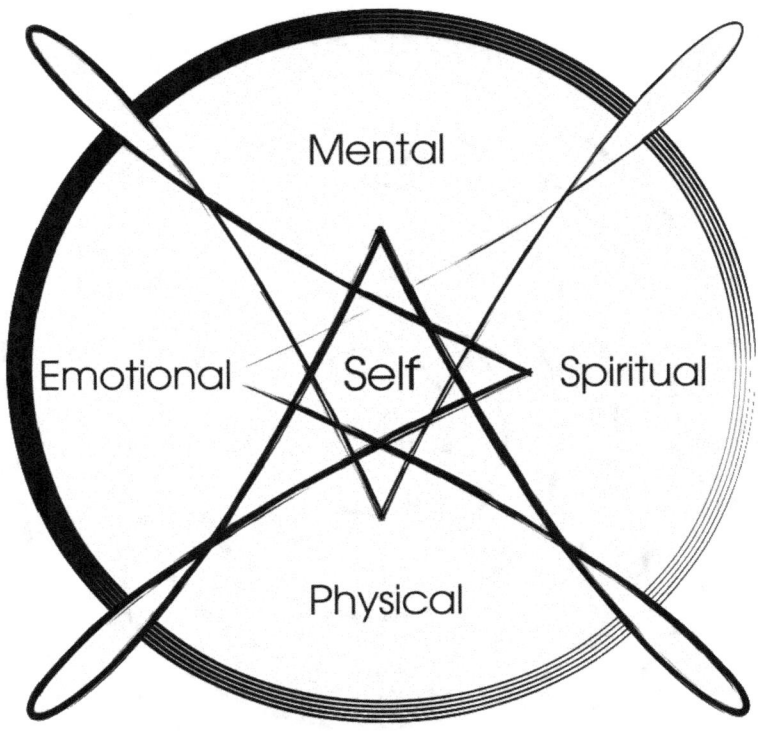

Figure 4. Four Aspects of the Self[iii]

This is also known as the "Four Directions Medicine Wheel." Each division corresponds to one of the four cardinal directions. The four aspects intersect at the centre where the 'self' is whole. These are artificial divisions of the interconnected reality of each person.

---

[1] Rheault, D'Arcy, "A Nation of Exclusion: Who Gets Left Out When We Talk About Canadian Culture (s)," in "New Visions of Nation: Re-Imagining Canadian Culture(s)," *Avancer, The Student Journal for the Study of Canada.* (Peterborough, Ontario: Trent University, 1998).

[2] Ibid.
[3] Ibid.

Bibliography

Written Works Cited

Benton-Banai, Edward. *The Mishomis Book, The Voice of the Ojibway.* Wisconsin: Indian Country Communications, 1988.

Black-Rogers, Mary. Forward to *Clothed-In-Fur and Other Tales: An Introduction to an Ojibwa World View* by T. Overholt and J. Baird Callicott. Lanham, MD: University Press of America, 1982.

Bourgeois, Paul. "An Ojibwe Conceptual Glossary." Major Glossary Paper (draft), TMs [photocopy], York University, February 26, 1998.

_____. "Odewegewin: An Ojibwe Epistemology." Major Paper (draft), TMs [photocopy], York University, March 31, 1998.

Brant Castellano, Marlene. "Updating Aboriginal Traditions of Knowledge." In *Indigenous Knowledge: Multiple Readings of Our World*, TMs [photocopy], 1-19. Toronto: University of Toronto Press, forthcoming, 1998.

Bruchac, Joseph, (ed.). *Native Wisdom*. San Francisco: HarperSanFrancisco, 1995.

Colorado, Pam. "Bridging Native and Western Science." *Convergence* XXI (2/3): 49-67. Toronto: International Council for Adult Education, 1988.

Couture, Joseph. "Native Studies and the Academy." In *Indigenous Knowledge* in *Global Context: Multiple Readings of Our World*, ed. George Dei, Buod Hall and Dorothy Goldin Rosenberg, TMs [photocopy], 1-14. Toronto: University of Toronto, forthcoming, 1998.

_____. "Next Time, Try an Elder!, 1979" TMs [photocopy].

_____. "The Role of Native Elders: Emergent Issues." In *The Cultural Maze: Complex Questions on Native Destiny in Western Canada*, ed. John Friesen, 201-217. Calgary: Detselig Enterprises, 1991.

_____. "Native Studies, Some Comments, April 1, 1993", TMs [photocopy]. Native Studies, Trent University, Peterborough, Ontario.

Deloria, Vine, Jr. *Red Earth White Lies*. New York: Skribner, 1995.

_____. *God is Red*. Colorado: Fulcrum, 1994.

_____. "American Indian Metaphysics." In *Winds of Change*. Boulder, Colorado: American Indian Science and Engineering Society, 1986. Quoted in Pam Colorado, "Bridging Native and Western Science." *Convergence* XXI (2/3): 49-67, Toronto, ON: International Council for Adult Education, 1988.

Dumont, James. "Journey To Daylight-Land Through Ojibwa Eyes". In *The First Ones: Readings in Indian/Native Studies*, ed. David Miller, 75-80. Saskatchewan: Saskatchewan Indian Federated College Press, 1992.

Guthrie, G.S., J.E. Raven and M. Schofield. *The Presocratic Philosophers, A Critical History with a Selection of Texts*, 2d ed. Cambridge: Cambridge University Press, 1983.

Hallowell, A. Irving. "Ojibwa Metaphysics of Being and the Perception of Persons." In *Person Perception and Interperson Behavior*, ed. R. Tagiuri and L Petoullo, 63-85. California: Stanford University, 1958.

_____. "Ojibwa Ontology, Behavior, and World View." In *Teachings from the American Earth* by Dennis Tedlock and Barbara Tedlock, (eds.). New York: Liveright, 1975.

Hill, Norbert S., Jr. (ed.). (Oneida). *Words of Power, Voices from Indian America*. Colorado: Fulcrum, 1994.

Johnston, Basil H., Forward to *Dancing with a Ghost, Exploring Indian Reality*, by Rupert Ross. Ontario: Octopus, 1992.

Nichols, John D. and Earl Nyholm. *A Concise Dictionary of Minnesota Ojibwe*. Minnesota: University of Minnesota Press, 1995.

Overholt, T. and J. Baird Callicott. *Clothed-In-Fur and Other Tales: An Introduction to an Ojibwa World View*. Lanham, Maryland: University Press of America, 1982.

Pettipas, Katherine. *Severing the Ties that Bind: Government Repression of Indigenous Religious Ceremonies in the Prairies*, Manitoba: University of Manitoba Press, 1994.

Pirsig, Robert. *Lila, An Inquiry Into Morals*. New York: Bantam Books, 1992.

Rheault, D'Arcy, "A Nation of Exclusion: Who Gets Left Out When We Talk About Canadian Culture (s)." In "New Visions of Nation: Re-Imagining Canadian Culture(s)," *Avancer, The Student Journal for the Study of Canada*. Peterborough, Ontario: Trent University, 1998.

Ross, Rupert. *Dancing with a Ghost, Exploring Indian Reality*. Ontario: Octopus, 1992.

Savard, Rémi. *Destin d'Amerique. Les Autochtones et nous.* Montréal: Édition de l'Hexagone, 1979.

Tedlock, Dennis and Barbara Tedlock, (eds.). *Teachings from the American Earth.* New York: Liveright, 1975.

Wong, Hertha Dawn. *Sending My Heart Back Across the Years, Tradition and Innovation in Native American Autobiography.* New York: Oxford University Press, 1992.

Interviews

Manitowabi, Edna. Interview by author, May 1997, Peterborough, Ontario. Tape recording. Tape in Edna Manitowabi's possession.

Conversations with Author

Beaudry, Dominic, (Odawa), 1998.

Bourgeois, Paul, (Ojibwe), 1997, 1998.

Elder, (Ojibwe), 1996.

Elder, (Ojibwe), 1997.

Longboat, Dan, (Kanienkehaka), 1998.

Manitowabi, Edna, (Odawa), 1997.

McInnis, Brian, (Ojibwe), 1998.

Osawamick, Florence, (Odawa), 1997.

Osawamick-Bourgeois, Lillian, (Odawa). 1998.

Traditional Teacher, (Odawa), 1996.

Traditional Teacher, (Ojibwe), 1995-1998

Traditional Teacher, (Ojibwe), 1997.

Workshop

Thrasher, Michael, (Métis), Workshop, Elders and Traditional Peoples Gathering, Trent University, Peterborough, Ontario, Canada, February 1995.

Further Readings

Agar, Michael. *Ethnography and Cognition.* USA: Burgess Publishing, 1974.

Ahenakew, F & H. C. Wolfart eds. & trans. *Kôhkominawak Otâcimowiniwâwa (Our Grandmothers' Lives as Told in their Own Words).* Saskatoon: Fifth House, 1992.

Albanese, Catharine L. *Nature Religion in America: From the Algonkian Indians to the New Age.* Chicago: University of Chicago press, 1990.

Alexander, Hartley Burr, (1873-1939). *The World's Rim: Great Mysteries Of The North American Indians.* Nebraska: University of Nebraska Press, 1953.

Anakomigenung (Andy Fields). "Anakomigenung's Medicine Lodge Parchment". Interview by Albert Reagan, (24 November, 1913). U. S. Department of Mines Geological Survey, Division of Anthropology, (B68 F3, no. 52) TMs [photocopy].

Arden, Harvey. *Wisdomkeepers: Meetings With Native American Spiritual Elders.* USA: Beyond Words, 1990.

Armstrong, Virginia Irving, ed. *I Have Spoken: American History Through the Voices of the Indians.* Chicago: The Swallow Press, 1986.

Babcock, Willoughby M. "The Grand Medicine Society of the Chippewa Indians". Minnesota: Minnesota State Historical Society, 1940.

Badger Tom. "A Psychological Interpretation of a Chippewa Origin Legend." Interview by Victor Barnouw (1944), *Journal of American Folk-lore* 68 (1955):73-217.

_____. "A Chippewa Mide Priest's Description of the Medicine Dance." Interview by Victor Barnouw (1944), *The Wisconsin Archeologist* 41 (1960): 77-97.

Barnouw, Victor, "A Psychological Interpretation of a Chippewa Origin Legend." *Journal of American Folklore* 68:73-85, 211-223, 341-355, 1955.

Beck, Peggy V. and Anna L. Walters. *The Sacred: Ways of Knowledge, Sources of Life.* Tsaile, AZ: Navajo Community College, 1977.

Benton-Banai, Edward. "The Seven Fires of the Ojibway Nation." November 1977. TMs [photocopy].

Black Elk. *The Sacred Pipe: Black Elk's Account of the Seven Rites of the Oglala Sioux.* Edited by Joseph E. Brown. Oklahoma: Norman: University of Oklahoma Press, 1953.

Black, Mary B. "Ocipwe Medicine Man as Barometer of Change." Transcript of speech presented at the Algonquian Conference, Green Bay, Wisconsin, 6 April, 1973. TMs [photocopy].

_____. *An Ethnoscience Investigation of Ojibwa Ontology and World View.* Ph.D. Dissertation, Stanford University. University Microfilms, 1967.

_____. Ojibwa Power Belief System. In *Anthropology of Power.* R. Rogelson and R. Adams, eds., London: Academic Press, 1977.

_____. "Ojibwa Questioning Etiquette and Use of Ambiguity." *Studies in Linguistics* 23 (1973).

_____. "Ojibwa Category Maskiki and the 'Power' System." TMs [photocopy].

Blessing, Fred K., Jr. *The Ojibway Indians Observed.* St. Paul, Minnesota: The Minnesota Archaeological Society, 1977.

_____. "Birchbark Mide Scrolls from Minnesota." *The Minnesota Archaeologist* 65/3 (1963): 91-142.

Bourgeois, Paul. "Midewiwin Music." Interview by Wendy Hawkin, (17 February, 1993). TMs [photocopy].

Boyer, Pascal. *Tradition As Truth And Communication: A Cognitive Description Of Traditional Discourse.* Cambridge: Cambridge University Press, 1990.

Brown, Dee. *Bury My Heart at Wounded Knee: An Indian History of the American West.* New York: Bantam Books, 1970.

Brown, J. S. H. & R. Brightman. *"The Order of the Dreamed": George Nelson on Cree and Northern Ojibwa Religion and Myth.* Winnipeg: The University of Manitoba Press, 1988.

Brown, Jennifer S. H. and Elizabeth Vibert, eds. *Reading Beyond Words, Contexts for Native History.* Peterborough, Ontario: Broadview Press, 1996.

Bunge, Robert. *An American Urphilosophie: An American Philosophy BP (Before Pragmatism).* Landham MD: University Press of America, 1984.

Bynum, David E. *The Dæmon in the Woods, A Study of Oral Narrative Patters.* Cambridge: The Centre for the Study of Oral Literature, 1978.

Cadzow, Donald A. "Bark Records of the Bungi Medéwin Society." *Indian Notes,* 1975.

Callicott, J. Baird. "American Indian Land Wisdom? Sorting Out the Issues", In *Defence of the Land Ethic: Essays in Environmental Philosophy,* Albany: State University of New York Press, 1989.

Calloway, Colin G., ed. *New Directions in American Indian History.* Oklahoma: University of Oklahoma Press, 1987.

Capps, Walter H. *Seeing with a Native Eye: Essays on Native American Religion.* New York: Harper & Row, 1976.

Carmody, Denis L. and John Tully Carmody. *Native American Religions: An Introduction.* New York: Paulist Press, 1993.

Chief Mack-E-Te-Be-Nessy (A.J. Blackbird). *History of the Ottawa and Chippewa Indians of Michegan.* Ypsilanti, Mich.: The Ypsilantian Printing House, 1887

Churchill, Ward. *Indians Are Us?: Culture and Genocide in Native North America Between the Lines,* Toronto, McClelland and Stewart, 1994.

Clark, Ella E. *Indian Legends of Canada.* Toronto: McClelland and Stewart, 1960.

Coleman, Bernard, Sr. "The Religion of the Ojibwa of Northern Minnesota." *Primitive Man* 10:33-57, 1937.

Copway, George. *The Traditional History and Characteristic Sketches of the Ojibway Nation.* London, UK: Charles Gilpin, 1850.

Dailey, Robert C. "The Midewiwin, Ontario's First Medical Society." *Ontario History* 50/3 (1958): 133-138.

Davidson, John F., "Ojibwa Songs." *Journal of American Folk-lore* 58:303-305.

Day-bway-wain-dung, "The Meaning of Certain Birch Bark Manuscripts of the Chippewa Medicine Men, Particularly those Belonging to Chief Day-bway-wain-dung, [with reproduction of figures]." Interview by Albert Reagan, (4 March, 1912). U.S. Department of Mines Geological Survey, Division of Anthropology, (no. 9). TMs [photocopy].

Deleary, Nicholas, "The Midewiwin, An Aboriginal Spiritual Institution: Symbols of Continuity: A Native Studies Culture-based Perspective." Masters Thesis, Carleton University, 1990.

Deloria, Vine, Jr. *Custer Died for Your Sins: An Indian Manifesto.* Collier-McMillan, 1969.

_____. *The Metaphysics of Modern Existence.* New York: Harper & Row, 1979.

Densmore, Frances. "An Ojibwa Prayer Ceremony." *Anthropologic Miscellanea* 9 (1907): 443-444.

_____. "Chippewa Customs." *Bureau of American Ethnology Bulletin* 86. Washington: Smithsonian Institution, 1929.

_____. *Chippewa Music.* Washington: Smithsonian Institution, Bureau of American Ethnology. Bulletin 45, 1910.

Dewdney, Selwyn. *The Sacred Scrolls of the Southern Ojibway.* Toronto: University of Toronto Press, 1975.

Dumont, James. "Rights and Ceremonies, The Midewiwin." Laurentian University, Sudbury, Ontario (NATI 2285EZ class notes), 1989. TMs [photocopy].

_____. "The Ojibway Medicine Dance, The Healing Dance of the Ojibway Midewiwin." Laurentian University, Sudbury, Ontario, 1989. TMs [photocopy].

Dupri, Wilhelm. *Religion In Primitive Cultures: A Study In Ethnophilosophy.* France: Mouton, 1975.

Durkheim, Emile. *Primitive Classification.* Chicago: University of Chicago Press, 1963.

Eliade, Mircea. *Cosmos and History: The Myth of the Eternal Return* (1949). New York: Harper and Brothers, 1959.

_____. *Shamanism: Archaic Techniques of Ecstacy.* New York: Pantheon, 1964.

_____. *The Quest: History and Meaning in Religion.* Chicago: The University of Chicago Press, 1969.

_____. *The Sacred and the Profane.* New York: Harcourt, Brace & World, 1959.

Erdoes, Richard and Olfonso Ortiz, eds. *American Indian Myths and Legends.* New York: Pantheon Books, 1984.

Erdoes, Richard. *Crying for a Dream: The World Through Native American Eyes.* Santa Fe, NM: Bear & Co., 1989.

Farella, John R. *The Main Stalk: A Synthesis of Navajo Philosophy.* Tucson: University of Arizona Press, 1984.

Fire, John and Richard Erdoes. *Lame Deer: Seeker of Visions.* New York: Simon and Schuster, 1972.

Geyshick, Ron and Judith Doyle. *Te Bwe Win* (Truth). Toronto: Impulse Editions, Summerhill Press, 1989.

Gill, Sam D. *Native American Religious Action: A Performance Approach to Religion.* Columbia: University of South Carolina Press, 1987.

Goody, Jack. *The Domestication Of The Savage Mind.* Cambridge: Cambridge University Press, 1977.

Hallowell, A. I. "Bear Ceremonialism in the Northern Hemisphere." *American Anthropologist* 28 no. 1 (1926): 1-175.

_____. "Ojibwa Personality and Acculturation." In *Social Structure and Personality: A Case Book.* Yeudhi A. Cohen, ed., New York: Holt Rhinehart and Winston, 1961.

_____. "Ojibwa World View and Disease." In *Man's Image in Medicine and Anthropology.* I. Goldston, ed., New York: International University Press, 1974.

_____. "Some Empirical Aspects of Northern Saulteaux Religion." *American Anthropologist* 36: 389-404, 1934.

Hamill, James Francis. *Ethno-Logic: The Anthropology Of Human Reasoning.* Illinois: University of Illinois Press, 1990.

Harringtom, M. R. "Religion and Ceremonies of the Lenepe." In *Indian Notes and Monogrraphs Pub. 19,* New York: Museum of the American Indian, Heye Foundation, 1921.

Harrison, Julia. "The Midewiwin: The Retention of An Ideology." Masters Thesis, University of Calgary, 1982.

Harrod, Howard, L. *Renewing the World: Plains Indian Religion and Morality.* Tucson: University of Arizona Press, 1987.

Henley, Thom. *Rediscovery: Ancient Pathways, New Directions: A Guide To Outdoor Education.* Western Canada Wilderness Committee, 1989.

Hickerson, H. "Some Implications of the Theory of the Particularity, or "Atomism", of Northern Algonkians." *Current Anthropology* 8: 313-343, 1967.

_____. "The Feast of the Dead Among the 17th C. Algonkians of the Upper Great Lakes." *American Anthropologist* 62: 81-107, 1960.

_____. "Notes on the Post-Contact Origin of the Midewiwin." *Ethnology* 9 no.4 (1963): 404-423.

Hoffman, W. J. "Notes on Ojibwa Folk-lore." *American Anthropologist* 2 (1889): 215-223.

_____. "Pictography and Shamanistic Rites of the Ojibwa." *American Anthropologist* 1 (1888): 209-229.

_____. "The Midê'wiwin or "Grand Medicine Society" of the Ojibwa." In *7th Annual Report of the Bureau of American Ethnology for the Years 1885-1886.* Washington: Smithsonian Institute, 1891, 143-300.

Hultkrantz, Ake. *Belief and Worship in Native North America.* Christopher Vecsey ed., Syracuse, NY: Syracuse University Press, 1981.

Indigenous Knowledge Systems And Development. University Press of America, 1980, [pamphlet].

Jackson, Michael. *Paths Toward A Clearing: Radical Empiricism And Ethnographic Inquiry.* Indiana: Indiana University Press, 1989.

James, B. J. "Some Critical Observations Concerning Analysis of Chippewa "Atomism" and Chippewa Personality." *American Anthropologist* 63: 721-746, 1961.

Johnston, Basil. *Ojibway Ceremonies.* Toronto: McClelland and Stewart, 1982.

_____. *Ojibway Heritage*. New York: Columbia University Press, 1976.

Jorgensen, Joseph G. *The Sun Dance Religion: Power for the Powerless.* Chicago: University of Chicago Press, 1972.

Josephy, Alvin M., ed.. *America in 1492: The World of the Indian Peoples Before the Arrival of Columbus.* New York: Vintage Books, 1993.

Kidd, Kenneth K. "A Radiocarbon Date on a Midewiwin Scroll from Burntside Lake, Ontario." *Ontario Archaeology* 35 (1981): 41-43.

_____. "Archaeological Investigations in Quetico Park, 1963." *Transactions of the Royal Canadian Institute,* vol.34, pt.2, no.71, 106-110.

King, J. H. C. *Thunderbird and Lightning, Indian Life in Northeastern North America 1600-1900.* London: British Museum Publications, 1982.

Koenig, Del M. "Cognitive Styles Of Indian, Metis, Inuit And Non-Natives Of Northern Canada And Alaska And Implications For Education." National Library of Canada, 1981. [pamphlet].

Landes, R. *Ojibwa Sociology.* New York: Columbia University Press, 1937a.

_____. "The Personality of the Ojibwa." *Character and Personality* 6: 51-60, 1937b.

_____. *Ojibwa Religion and the Midewiwin.* Madison: The University of Wisconsin Press, 1968.

Lawson, E. Thomas. *Rethinking Religion: Connecting Cognition and Culture.* Cambridge: Cambridge University Press, 1990.

Lerchs, Georges. Ottawa, Ontario, letter to J. Harrison, Calgary, Alberta, 27 November, 1979. TMs [photocopy].

Letter, from St. Clair Rapids, Ontario, 1834, From James —, concerning a Midewiwin Ceremony in that year, TMs [photocopy].

Letter, Raudot, 1770, Letter 47: Of the Saulteur Jugglers," TMs [photocopy].

Levi-Strauss, Claude. *Myth And Meaning: Five Talks For Radio.* Toronto: University of Toronto Press, 1978.

_____. *The Savage Mind* (1962). Chicago: The University of Chicago Press, 1966.

Loucks, Brian. *Indigenous Science, Development and Healing.* Department of Adult Education, Ontario Institute for Studies in Education, Toronto, 1990 (Fall), TMs [photocopy].

Mallery, Garrick. "Mide Song Records." *Bureau of American Ethnology*, 10th Annual Report, Smithsonian Institute, 1894, 229-257.

Mander, Jerry. *In the Absence of the Sacred: The Failure of Technology & The Survival of the Indian Nations.* San Francisco: Sierra Club Books, 1992.

Marks, Jay (aka Jamake Highwater). *The Primal Mind: Vision and Reality in Indian America.* New York: New American Library, 1981.

Martin, Pete. "Picture Writing of the Chippewa Indians, Peter Martin's Parchment, A Song [reproduction and explanation of figures]". Interview by Albert Reagan, *The Wisconsin Archeologist* 6/3 (1927): 81-82.

Maurer, Evan M. *The Native American Heritage.* Chicago: The Art Institute of Chicago, 1977.

McFadden, Steven S. H. *Profiles In Wisdom: Native Elders Speak About The Earth,* USA: Bear & Co., 1991.

Mills, Antonia and Richard Slobodin, eds. *American Rebirth: Reincarnation Belief Among North American Indians and Inuit.* Toronto: University of Toronto Press, 1994.

Morriseau, Norval. *Legends of My People The Great Ojibway*. Toronto: McGraw-Hill Ryerson, 1965.

Nabokov, Peter, ed. *Native American Testimony: A Chronicle of Indian-White Relations from Prophecy to the Present, 1492-1992*. New York: Viking, 1991.

Nett Lake, John (Farmer John). "Farmer John's Sky Manido Wigwam Medicine Lodge, [explanation of figures]." Interview by Albert Reagan, (20 April, 1914). U. S, Department of Mines Geological Survey, Division of Anthropology (no. 52e), TMs [photocopy]

Norman, Howard A. "Midé (Shaman) Picture Songs." *Ethnopoetics* 4 (1972): 28-30.

Paper, Jordan. ""Sweat Lodge": A Northern Native American Ritual for Communal Shamanistic Trance." *Temenos* 26 (1990): 85-94.

_____. "From Shaman to Mystic in Ojibwa Religion." *Studies in Religion* 9/2 (1980): 185-199.

_____. *Offering Smoke: The Sacred Pipe and Native American Religion*. Moscow: University of Idaho Press, 1988.

Parker, Arthur C. (Gawaso Wanneh), *The Indian How Book*. New York: Dover, 1975 (unabriged republication of 1931 edition).

Photos. 4 photos of Midewiwin Lodge, Sandy Lake, Ontario, 1973; 1 photo of Midewiwin Lodge, Berens River, Manitoba, 1915. (see description and personal account of Ceremony at Sandy Lake, Ontario in letter from Georges Lerchs to J. Harrison, 27 November, 1979). [photocopy].

Radin, Paul. "Ethnological Notes on the Ojibwa of Southeastern Ontario." *American Anthropologist* 30 (1928): 659-668.

_____. *Primitive Man As Philosopher*. USA: D. Appleton and Company, 1927.

Reagan, Albert B. "A Ritual Parchment and Certain Historical Charts of the Bois Fort Ojibwa of Minnesota." *Americana* 29 (1935): 228-244.

_____. "Picture Writing of the Chippewa Indians." *The Wisconsin Archeologist* 6/3 (1927): 81-82.

_____. "Some Notes on the Grand Medicine Society of the Bois Fort Ojibwa." *Americana* 27 (1933): 502-519.

Ritzenthaler, Robert E. and Pat Ritzenthaler. *The Woodland Indians of the Western Great Lakes.* Garden City, New York: The Natural History Press, 1970.

Ritzenthaler, Robert. "Chippewa Preoccupation with Health." *Bulletin, Milwaukee Public Museum* 19 part 4 (1953): 175-257.

_____. "The Ceremonial Destruction of Sickness by the Wisconsin Chippewa." *American Anthropologist* 47 (1945): 320-322.

Ross, A. C. (Ehanamani). *Mitakuye Oyasin (We Are All Related).* Denver, CO: Bear, 1989.

Roufs, Tim. "Myth in Method: More on Ojibwa Culture." *Current Anthropology* 15, no.3 (Sept. 1975): 307-309.

Seton, Ernest Thompson. *The Gospel Of The Redman: A Way Of Life.* Seton Village, 1966, 1963.

Sherzer, Joel and Anthony C. Woodbury, eds. *Native American Discourse, Poetics and Rhetoric.* Cambridge: Cambridge University Press, 1990.

Smithsonian Institution, Bureau of Ethnology. *Chippewa Indian Music, the Frances Densmore Collection.* Washington: Smithsonian, vol.1, 1983.

Steinmetz, Paul. *Meditations with Native Americans — Lakota Spirituality.* Santa Fe, NM: Bear & Company, 1972.

Tanner, Adrian. *Bringing Home Animals: Religious Ideology and Mode of Production of the Mistassini Cree Hunters.* St. John's: Memorial University of Newfoundland, 1974.

Tatahgausheke. "Farmer John, The Medicine Lodge Parchment." Interview by Albert Reagan, (20 April, 1914). U. S. Department of Mines Geological Survey, Division of Anthropology, (no 52b), TMs [photocopy].

_____. "The Historical Chart of the Migration of the Bois Fort Indians, Sugwaundugahwinninewug (Men of the Thick Fir Woods). Historical Sketch and Explanation of Chart Obtained by Albert B Reagan from Ta-ta-gaush-eke and Other Bois Fort Indians [reproduction of figures}." Interview by Albert Reagan, (20 April, 1914). U. S. Department of Mines Geological Survey, Division of Anthropology, (no 52d), TMs [photocopy].

The Sacred Tree. Four Worlds Development Press, Four Worlds Development Project, 1985.

Turner, Harold W. *Bibliography of New Religious Movements in Primal Societies. Volume II: North America.* Boston: G. K. Hall, 1978.

Vecsey, Christopher, ed. *Belief and Worship in Native North America.* Syracuse: Syracuse University Press, 1981.

_____. *Traditional Ojibwa Religion and Its Historical Changes.* Volume 152 in the series *Memoirs Series.* Philadelphia: American Philosophical Society, 1983.

Vennum, Thomas, Jr. "Ojibwa Origin-Migration Songs of the Mitewiwin." *Journal of American Folklore*, 1985.

Vizenor, Gerald, ed. *Narrative Chance, Postmodern Discourse on Native American Indian Literature.* Albuquerque: University of New Mexico Press, 1989.

Warren, William W. "Oral Traditions Respecting the History of the Ojibwa Nation." *Schoolcraft* 2 (1860): 135-167.

_____. "History of the Ojibways, Based Upon Traditions and Oral Statements." *Collections of the Minnesota Historical Society* 5:21-394, 1885.

Waugh, Earle H. and K. Dad Prithipaul. *Native Religious Traditions.* Studies in Religion, 8. Waterloo, ON: Wilfred Laurier University Press, 1979.

Waugh, F. W. "Midewiwin Notes 1919." TMs (Box 204R, Fld 20), 5 September 1919. Wabigoon, TMs [photocopy].